The Unofficial Buddhist

The Unofficial Buddhist
A Path Made by Walking

Robert Bluck

SHEFFIELD UK   BRISTOL CT

Published by Equinox Publishing Ltd.

UK: Office 415, The Workstation, 15 Paternoster Row, Sheffield, South Yorkshire S1 2BX

USA: ISD, 70 Enterprise Drive, Bristol, CT 06010

www.equinoxpub.com

First published 2025

© Robert Bluck 2025

All rights reserved. No part of this publication may be reproduced or transmitted in any form or by any means, electronic or mechanical, including photocopying, recording or any information storage or retrieval system, without prior permission in writing from the publishers.

ISBN-13 978 1 80050 570 4 (hardback)
         978 1 80050 571 1 (paperback)
         978 1 80050 572 8 (ePDF)
         978 1 80050 668 8 (ePub)

British Library Cataloguing-in-Publication Data

A catalogue record for this book is available from the British Library.

Library of Congress Cataloging-in-Publication Data

Names: Bluck, Robert, 1947–, author.
Title: The Unofficial Buddhist : A Path Made by Walking / Robert Bluck.
Description: Bristol : Equinox Publishing Ltd, 2025. | Includes bibliographical references. | Summary: "This book explores Buddhist-inspired teaching and practice for today's secular world—but outside the monastic traditions of Buddhism. If you have been practising Buddhism without finding a local centre where you feel comfortable—or if you are outside Buddhism, but looking in with interest—you are probably an unofficial Buddhist yourself. If so, this book is for you"—Provided by publisher.
Identifiers: LCCN 2025020357 (print) | LCCN 2025020358 (ebook) | ISBN 9781800505704 (hardback) | ISBN 9781800505711 (paperback) | ISBN 9781800505728 (pdf) | ISBN 9781800506688 (epub)
Subjects: LCSH: Dharma (Buddhism) | Conduct of life—Religious aspects—Buddhism.
Classification: LCC BQ4190 .B58 2025 (print) | LCC BQ4190 (ebook) | DDC 294.3/444--dc23/eng/20250620
LC record available at https://lccn.loc.gov/2025020357
LC ebook record available at https://lccn.loc.gov/2025020358

Typeset by JS Typesetting Ltd, Porthcawl, Mid Glamorgan

In grateful memory of Trevor Ling

Contents

Acknowledgements	ix
Introduction	1
Part One: Drawing the Map	
1 Four Truths – or Four Tasks?	9
2 Looking for the Middle Way	17
3 Finding a Local Path	30
4 Towards a Zen Path?	40
Part Two: Walking the Path	
5 Taking the First Steps	53
6 Cultivating Compassionate Behaviour	61
7 The Power of Speech	76
8 And What Do *You* Do for a Living?	84
9 Focusing on the Present	89
10 Skilful Meditation	100
11 A Path towards Wisdom?	115
12 All Together Now	124
Appendix: Verses for Meditation and Reflection	133
Notes	139
Bibliography	145

Acknowledgements

Those who helped me write this book include former and current teachers, guides and spiritual friends. I am particularly grateful to the late Professor Trevor Ling, for his lectures and kindness to struggling students; and much more recently to Professor Peter Harvey, whose thorough supervision of my doctoral thesis was a model of friendly exploration.

I would like to thank all my Buddhist teachers. Ajahn Sumedho, Ajahn Munindo and other Theravada Forest Sangha monks and nuns offered timely guidance. Revd Master Daishin Morgan and other Soto Zen monks and nuns similarly supported my practice. Stephen and Martine Batchelor's secular Buddhism retreat and online Secular Dharma course were both inspirational.

Discussions with all my wise and compassionate Buddhist friends have made a significant contribution. I would particularly like to thank Bob Adshead, Linda France, Annie Harrison, Joan Matthews, Alex Reed and Jenny Rookes. I am also grateful to those who read and commented on early drafts, answered my queries, or steered me away from foolish mistakes. These include Revd Dr Nicholas Buxton, Revd Dr Ian Duffield, Phil Hanson, Carrie Harris, Ellie Ling, Christopher Sell, and Revd Canon Gavin Wort. Special thanks go to George Hepburn, Joan Matthews and Walter Young for their helpful feedback on specific chapters – and to Nicholas Buxton for his generous endorsement.

Beyond acknowledgement or thanks, there is my patient and precious Caroline.

Introduction

What is an unofficial Buddhist? Someone whose monastery is their living room! Many in the West practise in Theravada, Tibetan or Zen traditions, visiting monasteries and groups attached to them. But there are also many who choose not to commit themselves to one of these 'official' schools. Perhaps they have no local Buddhist centre, or have not found any nearby centres or online groups appealing – or maybe they are wary of organized religion in general.

These 'unofficial Buddhists' practise either with a few friends or on their own. In both Europe and North America, they may make up the largest number of *convert* Buddhists – those outside Asian immigrant traditions – though they are often unaware of each other's existence. But 'unofficial' doesn't mean ambivalent or uncommitted. These practitioners may be just as dedicated as those following the monastic traditions. They have been called Buddhism's 'new pioneers', exploring the inner territory of how to practise in the modern world in a way which is still true to the Buddha's original teaching.

There is a wide range of these unofficial Buddhists. Some might be called 'free-range Buddhists', based within one tradition but valuing the teaching and practice of others – visiting Theravada groups, reading the Dalai Lama's books, or attending Zen retreats. Others support new Buddhist organizations which have adapted or blended elements from one or more traditions, for example Vipassana groups or the Triratna community. Some have consciously discarded 'religious' elements of Buddhism, such as monastic-based ritual and devotional practice, and would call themselves 'secular Buddhists'. And there are those we might call 'not-just-Buddhists', such as Zen Catholics and Quaker Buddhists, with dual or even multiple spiritual identities.

People *outside* Buddhism may also find the Buddha's teaching has something valuable to offer them. Perhaps they practise mindfulness meditation and wish to explore its Buddhist background. Their concern for the environment and social justice may draw them towards what has been called 'engaged Buddhism'. These 'Buddhist-leaning' people may be Christians or Jews or even secular humanists. This is not as unusual as it seems, since the Buddha described his teaching as 'directly visible ... inviting one to come and see ... to be personally experienced by the wise'.[1] You don't have to be a Christian to love your neighbour, and you don't have to be a Buddhist to practise loving-kindness meditation!

So if you've been practising Buddhism without finding a local centre or online group where you feel comfortable, or if you're outside Buddhism, but looking in with interest – you're probably an unofficial Buddhist yourself. If so, this book is for you.

The Buddha's teaching addresses the human situation, offering ways of relieving the suffering we experience individually and collectively. The Covid-19 pandemic has brought home to us the scale of human suffering, and the fact that our personal safety and well-being is intimately connected to the safety and well-being of everyone else. Buddhism's core principles of compassion, tolerance and interconnectedness stand in contrast to the fragmented individualism we often see today in both self-centred greed and communal discord. The Buddha has something to teach us all.

Please don't get me wrong. I'm not trying either to convert people to Buddhism, or to tempt Buddhists away from the Theravada or Tibetan or Zen monastic traditions, if they are happy within them. Having practised in two of these traditions for many years, I have a profound respect for the monks and nuns and lay people who have supported my own practice in many ways. But now I need to find a different way to follow the Buddha's teaching. I'm definitely an unofficial Buddhist.

The question I began with was simple: How should we practise as Buddhists in our largely secularized Western world? More broadly, we might ask: How can the Buddha's ancient teaching support our lives in this modern world, whether we are Buddhists or Christians, religious or secular? These are the questions this book attempts to answer.

* * *

When I first became a Buddhist, bewildered friends asked me what it was all about, and I often quoted a verse from the *Dhammapada*: *Avoid doing evil, learn to do good, purify your own heart.*[2] Sadly this confused them even more. They thought it sounded much too simple, suspiciously like the Ten Commandments, and with a weird bit on the end. What would it mean to purify your heart?

Buddhism tends to avoid black-and-white categories like *good* and *evil*. Buddhists prefer to talk about what is wise or foolish, beneficial or harmful, skilful or unskilful. This helps us consider our actions in terms of their effect on other people, as well as on our own minds, rather than an abstract wish to shun evil and do good. With a nod to the Zen precepts we'll be meeting later on, another way of expressing this verse might be: *Avoid all harmful actions of body, speech and mind; practice skilful actions of body, speech and mind; awaken your compassionate heart.* This still leaves us to work out which actions are which, how to avoid harmful ones and develop skilful ones, and how meditation can help us to awaken our compassionate heart. But it's a start. Of course describing the teaching is usually much easier than following it!

Wanderer, there is no path: the path is made by walking ...

These words are carved on a forty-foot-long stone seat in the Garden of Reflection at Wells Cathedral. I came across them on my way to a Secular Buddhism retreat, and they seemed appropriate for the occasion. This quotation is from the Spanish poet Antonio Machado (1875–1939): *Wanderer, your footsteps are the path, and nothing more. Wanderer, there is no path, the path is made by walking ... there is no path – only your wake in the sea.*[3]

This retreat was a very significant one for me. It was led by the Buddhist teachers and authors Stephen and Martine Batchelor, each with a decade's training in monastic traditions as a former monk and nun. Throughout a week spent in silence, we alternated between sitting and walking meditation, with evening dharma talks from Stephen and Martine. After the first sitting meditation, we spread out into the grounds on a hot sunny morning, and I found a shady spot under an oak tree. Walking slowly back and forth, with steps matching the rhythm of my breathing, half an hour seemed to pass quickly. Soon it was time for sitting meditation again.

Each time we came outside, some people would wander in the grounds, do a little gentle yoga, or rest before the next sitting. I went back to my spot under the tree, walking up and down. As the week wore on, wandering or stretching or resting became more and more attractive. But I kept coming back to the dappled sunshine under the oak leaves. Twelve small steps, taken slowly, and then turning around to walk back again. Soon there was a line in the rough grass under the tree, and by the end of the week this line had become a path – a path made by walking.

Perhaps we need a middle way between doggedly maintaining traditional elements which no longer feel relevant, and diluting traditional teaching and practice so much that it becomes unrecognisable. If we keep strictly to the Asian cultural norms of Theravada, Tibetan or Zen Buddhist traditions, we will always be chanting in Pali or Tibetan or Japanese rather than in English. If we simply meditate for a few minutes each day, along the lines of contemporary secular mindfulness, we may be absorbed into the cult of personal well-being, a cornerstone of Western consumer capitalism.

This book explores how to find a middle way between these two extremes, and then to practise it, coming to terms with the suffering we inevitably experience, dealing with our habitual reactions, and cultivating the Buddha's ancient path of morality, meditation and wisdom in our modern society. Each chapter will begin with a different question, and then attempt to answer it.

* * *

Part One: Drawing the Map attempts to look for and define that middle way, as the Buddha often recommended, but not just between over-indulgence and hair-shirt asceticism. These four chapters attempt to map out where the path might start from, and what shape it might take. (The original title was 'Secular Zen', but I realized this conflated two more 'official' terms: unofficial Buddhists are not necessarily secular, and their practice may not fit neatly within the Zen tradition.)

Chapter 1 addresses what Stephen Batchelor has called a 'fourfold task', revising and interpreting the Buddha's Four Noble Truths for our modern secular age. This will involve seeing and accepting things as they are – rather than as we would like them to be – and letting go of our habitual reactions to whatever comes our way. If we can observe this process, we are ready to begin cultivating the path itself.

With this in mind, Chapter 2 seeks to find a middle way between Asian and Western culture, between ancient and modern worldviews, and between religious and secular approaches. Trying to avoid religious dogmatism – and its counterpart in an equally rigid secularism – will include considering where to look for reliable guidance on how to put the Buddha's teaching into practice.

Chapter 3 is a more personal look at how this might work out at a local level, wherever you happen to be – in my case as a Buddhist in Britain – and how this 'unofficial Buddhism' may be able to draw on elements in the local spiritual heritage.

Chapter 4 asks which of the existing traditions might be most helpful for unofficial Buddhists. While some elements of Theravada and Tibetan Buddhism are appropriate, the Zen tradition may prove more flexible, since it can be practised by Buddhists and non-Buddhists alike. But Zen in the West may be very different from Zen in Japan!

* * *

Part Two: Walking the Path explores in detail the various elements of the Buddha's path of morality, meditation and wisdom, often using the Zen precepts as a guide. There are practical suggestions at each stage – taking the first steps and then developing our practice – walking the path for ourselves.

Chapter 5 examines how to take these first steps, with an initial confidence that there is a path to follow, and an initial understanding of the Buddhist view of the world. The Buddha listed ten wise and unwise actions, later developed into the moral precepts all Buddhists try to follow. This is not simply a moral code, as these precepts also invite us to become more aware of our habitual unskilful patterns of speech, actions and thought, and so learn gradually to let go of them.

The next three chapters describe a path towards wise and compassionate behaviour, as an essential element of spiritual practice. Chapter 6 focuses on our actions, where we are encouraged to avoid harming or exploiting others, and to let go of our own obsessional behaviour – developing loving-kindness instead of aggression, generosity instead of grasping, contentment instead of over-indulgence, and mindfulness instead of intoxication. Chapter 7 deals with speech, encouraging us to avoid false, malicious, harsh and useless speech, and to develop instead a pattern of truthful, kindly, gentle and helpful communication with others. Chapter 8 examines how we can extend this wise and compassionate behaviour into our working lives, choosing beneficial rather than harmful ways to earn a living, and using our income as best we can to support other people and protect the environment.

Two chapters then attempt to find a path towards developing both mindfulness in our daily lives and a regular practice of formal meditation. Chapter 9 focuses on the skilful effort and mindfulness which can support our meditation throughout our daily lives, when we are able to let go of negative states of mind, developing positive mental states instead. Chapter 10 suggests how four specific meditation practices can develop both our mental equilibrium and our compassionate response to others. The most commonly used is mindfulness of breathing, but meditations on loving-kindness and on gratitude, as well as walking meditation, are also described.

Chapter 11 outlines how this sustained practice of both regular meditation and compassionate behaviour – gradually turning our habitual greed, hatred and delusion into generosity, loving-kindness and insight – can lead to a new understanding of ourselves and the world around us. We may think of this awareness as wisdom, awakening, enlightenment, or even nirvana – or simply as being more peaceful.

Chapter 12 has suggestions about how all of this might be put together in our daily practice, both as individuals and as a community or sangha, still as unofficial Buddhists rather than in any new 'Buddhist movement'.

For readers who might value a simple form of words to aid this process, an appendix includes verses which can be used to prepare the mind for meditation, and to renew our commitment.

*　*　*

This is a book about Buddhist *practice*. If you want to learn about Buddhist history or philosophy, or the teachings of different schools of Buddhism – all of which are well worth studying – many other books are available. (Those I have drawn on are listed in the bibliography as a small sample of a huge literature.) This book is less about what we learn or what we believe – though developing understanding and confidence is part of it – and more about how we speak and act, how we spend our time at home and at work, and how we can establish and maintain a meditation practice. Each chapter contains ideas and suggestions, rather than a set of instructions to follow. I hope you find something here to help you navigate your own spiritual path, whether or not you choose to call yourself a Buddhist – official or unofficial.

Part One

Drawing the Map

Chapter 1

Four Truths – or Four Tasks?

Let's begin with Gotama, who lived five centuries before Jesus in a northern India very different from modern Western society, and who became known as the Buddha after his experience of awakening. What did he teach, and is his teaching still relevant today?

The First 'Sermon'

Introductory books on Buddhism often begin with an account of Gotama's early life – his sheltered upbringing, his sudden awareness of the extent of human suffering, and the fruitless years of ascetic practice before his famous awakening under the bodhi tree. Then comes a statement about what happened next: *In his first sermon in the deer park at Sarnath, the Buddha taught the Four Noble Truths to his five former ascetic companions.* This simple sentence locates and describes the very beginning of what we now call Buddhism – but it can be somewhat misleading. The nature and content of this initial meeting may have been rather different from what is commonly supposed and repeatedly described.

To start with, this probably wasn't a formal *sermon*, with a preacher talking to a passive audience. The Buddha's discourses were usually less formal. His listeners would often interrupt, or he would put questions to them, using the same method as his near contemporary Socrates. In the *Kalama Sutta*, for example, he asks his audience: 'What do you think, Kalamas? When greed ... hatred ... delusion arises in a person, is it for his welfare or his harm? ... Are these things wholesome or unwholesome?'[1]

Most of the discourses might be seen instead as teaching sessions, more like tutorials or seminars than lectures, though with a practical rather than an academic approach. The Buddha is sometimes portrayed in the texts as an authoritative (or even omniscient) purveyor of truth, but he always took care to *engage* with his audience, using examples or similes from their own experience as farmers or skilled artisans. This level of engagement is less common in modern Buddhist teaching, where dharma talks at monasteries are usually much more like sermons than seminars, with monks or nuns addressing a silent audience, perhaps with a few minutes for questions at the end.

The Four Noble Truths are often described by academic and popular writers as 'the essence of the doctrine' or 'the cornerstone of Buddhist doctrine'. This invites Western readers into familiar territory. Doctrines are things we are expected to *believe* – so Buddhism must be another religion, albeit an unusual one, without a central divine being or creator god. If I tell people I'm a Buddhist, they often ask: What do Buddhists *believe*? When I try to explain that Buddhism is really more about *practice* than belief, they look at me with suspicion, as if I can't even answer a simple question about my own religion. (Of course *all* religions are about practice: the popular misconception that equates religion with *belief* can probably be blamed on Protestant Christianity – but that's another story.)

Despite what modern writers keep telling us, the Buddha explained repeatedly to monastics and lay people that his teaching is *not* a set of doctrines to be accepted without question, but something to be examined and tested in their own experience. A crucial term in the discourse quoted in the Introduction is *ehipassika*, 'inviting one to come and see' – or in other words 'look for yourselves' – very different to the divine revelation of Truth (with a capital T) offered by many spiritual teachers.[2]

The standard account of the Four Noble Truths describes them as statements made by the Buddha to the effect that:

1 life is suffering;
2 this suffering is caused by craving or desire;
3 this suffering can be brought to an end; and
4 there is an eightfold path which will lead to the end of this suffering.

This account is often repeated, but again it can be misleading. When commentators tell us the Buddha's first and most important teaching is 'life is suffering', it's not surprising that Buddhism is sometimes seen as pessimistic. The scholar and translator Edward Conze (1904–79) declared that 'Buddhists take an extremely gloomy view of the conditions in which we have the misfortune to live.'[3] You don't have to meet many Buddhists to realize that this generalization is highly inaccurate! The Pali word *dukkha* is far broader than 'suffering', in the sense of physical and mental anguish. It's better translated as 'unsatisfactoriness', reflecting the impermanence of our human existence and everything to do with it. We want everything to *last* – including ourselves and our precious belongings. *Dukkha* reflects the frustration we often feel when things are not as we wish them to be.

The Buddha did *not* teach that 'life' is *dukkha*, but that birth, old age, disease, death, and the ever-changing aspects of the human experience are all *dukkha*.[4] This is not just splitting hairs. Yes, every aspect of human existence has an element of unsatisfactoriness about it, if only because it's impermanent. We want to remain young, healthy and immortal, but inevitably we all grow old, we get sick, and we die. But to say that '*life* is suffering' equates human life as a whole with the condition of suffering, saying in effect: 'life is *only* suffering'. We know this is nonsense. Our lives can be full of joy as well as misery, and most of the time full of something in between, which we tend to call normal life.

Moreover, 'life is suffering' is a *metaphysical* statement, one which cannot be shown to be true by either evidence or reasoning. People often asked the Buddha metaphysical questions: Is the universe eternal or not? Is the soul different from the body? Do we exist after death or not? Really hard ones! The Buddha either remained silent or expressed a lack of interest in such questions. They don't relate to the human predicament and how to solve it.

Instead of being doctrinal *statements*, the Four Noble Truths are closely linked in the Pali texts to specific *actions* which the Buddha said needed to be undertaken. The first noble truth needs to be understood, the second to be abandoned, the third to be realized, and the fourth to be developed.[5] But this doesn't make sense! It's not the *truth* about *dukkha* which needs to be understood, but *dukkha* itself. It's not the *truth* about the cause which needs to be abandoned, but the cause itself. The Pali word *sacca* may be translated as 'reality' rather than 'truth', so perhaps we need to respond appropriately to these four *realities* rather than believing in four *truths*. 'Suffering' needs to be understood; its origin (whether we call it craving or desire or something else) needs to be abandoned; the 'fading and cessation' of this craving needs to be realized; and the eightfold path needs to be cultivated.

After Buddhism

Stephen Batchelor (b. 1953) develops these ideas in his book *After Buddhism*, which has had a deep effect on my own understanding. He describes the Four Noble Truths as a *fourfold task* rather than doctrinal assertions. This is what first attracted me to Buddhism – as something you *do* rather than something you *believe*. Batchelor argues that the distinction has been partially obscured by centuries of monastic tradition, gradually erecting a belief system around the central task of spiritual practice. (And as a recovering academic, I admit that reading and writing about Buddhism is sometimes more interesting than practising meditation and compassionate behaviour.)

The question addressed in *After Buddhism* is the same as mine: 'What does it mean to practice the dharma of the Buddha in the context of modernity?'[6] As he treated metaphysical questions as irrelevant, the Buddha's teaching can hardly be expressed in terms of claims about eternal truth. Instead of trying to pin down abstract ideas about right and wrong, we should focus on acting wisely and compassionately in each situation we face. But the traditional Buddhist view of the world still relies on an ancient Indian metaphysics and cosmology, which can seem very far distant from our modern scientific materialism. This suggests that we may need to develop instead what Batchelor calls 'a coherent, ethical, contemplative, and philosophical vision of the dharma for our secular age'.[7]

Batchelor draws a distinction between 'religious Buddhists', whose practice is based on *beliefs*, and 'secular Buddhists', who focus instead on *questions* and how to respond to them. The dharma can be practised in *this world* rather than hoping for a favourable rebirth in the future, with the emphasis on easing suffering for all beings rather than on personal enlightenment. This doesn't mean reducing the dharma to a self-help manual: a secular Buddhism still has the 'religious' quality of being 'rooted in "ultimate concerns"'.[8] But this needs to focus on practice rather than theory, learning how to change our behaviour, rather than accumulating knowledge for its own sake.

A secular approach to Buddhism builds on earlier ideas. As Religious Studies emerged from Christian Theology as a new discipline, one of its pioneers, Trevor Ling (1920–95), suggested that Buddhism began as a potentially new form of culture or civilization, which over time became organized into a major Indian religion.[9] It could be argued that the

Buddha's original teaching gradually became a set of orthodoxies, where the Four Noble Truths became seen as *facts* rather than *tasks*, springing from a growing view of the Buddha as omniscient as well as enlightened. If we leave aside the ideas shared with Brahminism, such as karma and rebirth, we may instead be left with what Stephen Batchelor describes as 'four central ideas ... the *principle* of conditionality ... the *practice* of a fourfold task ... the *perspective* of mindful awareness ... [and] the *power* of self-reliance'.[10]

This is not to say that the Buddha was a modern secularist. He lived in a radically different religious context to our own. We should not put on 'secular' spectacles to make his teaching look like modern secularism; but neither should we wear 'religious' spectacles to make his teaching look like other religions. As the goal of the Buddhist path, nirvana has often been portrayed as a distant prospect, which committed practitioners may eventually reach in a future lifetime. The Buddha hints that it may actually be closer at hand and 'directly visible, immediate' – but only when we have completely abandoned our habitual reactions of greed, hatred and delusion.[11] This is the fourfold task to be undertaken.

Four Tasks

Firstly, we need to recognize *dukkha* as simply being *the way things are* – the situations we dislike, the things we want but cannot have, and the loved ones we lose. If we can accept and even embrace life as it really is, complete with its joy and sadness, we can learn to let go of our greed, hate and delusion, and become more generous and compassionate, and hopefully less confused. With practice we can accept the situation we're in at any moment – a happy meeting with friends or even an angry confrontation with someone. This brings a certain stillness, allowing us to become more aware of what's happening, rather than being overwhelmed by our emotional responses, our desires and aversions, our hopes and fears.

Secondly, we need to let go of *dukkha* as it arises. We are usually attracted to what seems pleasant, averse to what seems unpleasant, and bored with what seems neutral. These reactions aren't good or bad: they are just what happens when we see and hear things around us. The cause of *dukkha* is said to be *tanha*, often given as *desire* or *craving*, but better translated as *thirst* – something built into the fabric of our human existence. Rather than one simply *causing* the other, it is perhaps more that they *arise together* – the thirst for what seems pleasant, and the unsatisfactoriness of not getting hold of it. To let go of our habitual and almost instinctive responses, we have to get beyond viewing everything as nice or nasty or boring, training ourselves instead to recognize our precarious situation in a world where suffering is always present. If we can do this, our habitual reactions will tend to fade away as we begin to see them as less important, less insistent, even trivial perhaps.

These reactions to what we see and hear often spring from the familiar elements of greed, hatred and delusion. I like *these* people and want to be close to them; I dislike *those* people and want to be far away from them; and *my* beliefs and opinions are the right ones. So these reactions are really all about *me* – *me* at the centre of things, *me* getting what *I* want. That's why the reactions are so hard to let go of. Our fears and anxieties just won't go away, and we seem unable to change the way we feel. But these natural reactions need not define us. When we see another person who is suffering, we can also naturally react with understanding and kindness. It is futile to deny this process of our habitual reactions, and often impossible to stop it: as Batchelor suggests, letting it go may just mean letting it be.[12]

Thirdly, the way our reactions can fade needs to be *observed*. Each time our habitual greed or hatred or delusion falls away, even briefly, we can look closely at what is happening, and enjoy that moment of freedom. Watching the process helps us to understand our pattern of reactions, and to appreciate the moments when we can think, speak and act in this free space. Whenever this happens, we can observe that our emotional response – that strong feeling of anger or fear or frustration – has disappeared, because we have let go of it, and allowed it to subside. Batchelor argues that 'one can become aware of nirvana *whenever* greed, hatred, and confusion are momentarily inactive', and that such awareness need not be limited to Buddhists or meditators.[13]

Finally, the eightfold path needs to be followed as a practical model for our lives rather than a theoretical ideal of piety. Batchelor warns that it needs to be *cultivated*, 'created and sustained from moment to moment' with effort and care. It's not winding into the distance 'waiting for you to take a leisurely stroll along it'.[14] It is a path made by walking. While traditional Buddhist teaching sometimes focuses on how to escape from the endless cycle of birth and death, these four tasks encourage us to engage directly with our suffering world – rather than worrying about noble truths – and to respond with compassion.

What we are cultivating here is our own lives, with a growing carefulness about our own actions, for the way we speak and think and behave in our relationships with other people. This is the middle way, the path we make for ourselves by being aware of everything we experience. It changes the way we see the world. Like a skilful gardener, we move beyond the theoretical information we have acquired through study, and gradually gain the practical skill of cultivation – the 'know-how' rather than the knowledge. We are responsible for our own actions and speech and thinking, prompted by our own experience rather than dictated by an external authority.

Doctrine or Practice?

Although *dharma* is often translated as 'truth', the Buddha's discourses don't present these terms as synonyms: his teaching is always ethical rather than metaphysical, to do with action rather than belief. Batchelor sees the focus on truths rather than tasks as emphasizing 'abstract knowledge over felt experience'. He argues that even using the term 'noble truths' supports 'doctrinal belief over practical application'.[15] The distinction between conventional and ultimate truth is often assumed by commentators, though the Buddha himself used neither of these terms. This view of 'two truths' may have lent institutional authority to a monastic elite who could then claim that they alone had access to a deeper understanding of the Buddha's teaching.

Despite many innovations in both Theravada and Mahayana Buddhism over the centuries, there has also been an influential element of conservatism, a wish to retain ancient teachings and practices, and a resistance to change. Like many other religious organizations, Buddhist monastic traditions have sometimes tended to construct a system of religious beliefs which is safe from criticism, rather than developing the ability to respond to situations as they arise, free from fixed opinions and habitual reactions. Batchelor suggests that this is an 'outdated Buddhist dogma' which needs to be abandoned, to 'rethink the dharma' and create new Buddhist communities to practise the fourfold task together.[16] A secular sangha would replace the monastic hierarchy with a Quaker-like model which values all members equally and operates through consensus rather than imposed authority. In such a group of spiritual friends, individuals can offer each other mutual support and commitment. The challenge is to create and develop 'a sangha based on communal, dharma-oriented principles', steering a path between an authoritarian hierarchy and an isolating individualism.[17]

Perhaps Batchelor is being rather too hard on the monastic tradition. Conservatives are of course those who *conserve*, as well as those who tend to resist change. Without the monastic conservation of the dharma, it would surely have ceased to exist. And although the monastic hierarchy may have evolved partly to secure and protect its own status, this is what often happens as organizations gradually become institutions. There's also the risk that a secularized Buddhism may lead to discarding elements simply because they appear too *religious*. If we abandon chanting or bowing, for example, because we associate them with a pious attitude, we are again following our own habitual reactions, rather than examining these reactions and allowing them to fade.

* * *

Before we begin to explore this eightfold path, there's more navigation to be done. We need to find a path which leads between Asian and Western culture, between religious and secular approaches, and between relying exclusively on monastic authority or personal experience. Can we find a middle way between the habitual over-indulgence which our consumer society constantly encourages, and a hair-shirt asceticism which ignores the everyday situations we find ourselves in? That's what the Buddha recommended, when he found that neither of these two extremes led to awakening. Can we find a path that leads through our own local territory, our own cultural and spiritual background, whatever that may be? And could one of the existing Buddhist traditions – perhaps with appropriate adaptations for our contemporary world – be a helpful guide to cultivating the eightfold path? These are the questions to be explored in the next three chapters.

Chapter 2

Looking for the Middle Way

The young Gotama lived a life of extremes. As the son of a local ruler, he was brought up in relative luxury, sheltered from human suffering, at least compared with the subsistence farmers all around him. When he suddenly encountered an old man, a sick man, and a corpse being taken to cremation, he was deeply shocked. Inspired by the calm demeanour of a wandering ascetic, he chose to leave his family, including his wife and baby son, to seek a solution to the prospect of old age, sickness and death. For six years he practised with various teachers, and finally adopted a rigidly strict asceticism. But this offered no more escape than the self-indulgent youth he had previously enjoyed. Finally, seated in prolonged meditation under a pipal tree, he had a transformative experience often referred to as *enlightenment*, after which he became known as the Buddha, the one who is *awakened*. He spent the rest of his life teaching what he called the *middle way* between luxury and asceticism.

How can we find a helpful middle way in today's world? Not just between indulgence and renunciation – but between ancient Asian and modern Western worldviews, with their different cultural backgrounds. Can we steer a middle course between 'religious' and 'secular' approaches, with their different attitudes to centralized authority and personal experience?

Asian and Western Culture

As Buddhism spread into South-east Asia, China, Tibet and Japan, the original Indian flavour of teaching and practice gradually merged with the existing religion and culture of each new country, so that Theravada Buddhism in Sri Lanka and Thailand and Myanmar, Tibetan Buddhism, and Japanese Zen all have quite different flavours. This process is common to most religions, but more evident in Buddhism, where the absence of a divine creator or a sacred scripture allows variations to develop more easily. These different expressions of Buddhism have been imaginatively described as 'the gift-wrapping round the Buddha's gift', which may look quite different from the gift itself.

In the twentieth century Buddhism found its way into Western countries, and we now have various forms of Theravada, Tibetan and Zen traditions in much of Europe, North America and Australasia. As these forms gradually become embedded, a similar accommodation with this new context will inevitably occur, perhaps with ever-increasing diversity. Many Western Buddhists, particularly immigrants from Asian communities, continue to practise in traditional Asian forms. Many others – and perhaps a majority of convert Buddhists – are unaffiliated, practising on their own or with independent groups.

So people drawn towards Buddhist practice have a wide variety of choices. We could decide to join a traditional Asian form of Theravada, Tibetan or Zen Buddhism. Each has its own monastic core of authoritative teachers, its own formal rules and rituals and devotional practices. Each operates wholly or partly in its own language, whether Thai, Tibetan, or Japanese. In Asian countries these have long been separate traditions with a wide appeal across social classes, and their strong sense of spiritual cohesion can now be seen in some Asian immigrant communities. But convert Buddhists may feel uncomfortable within these traditional forms, elements of which can seem culturally alien.

Christians and humanists and others interested in the Buddha's teaching are unlikely to sign up as official Buddhists. These 'Buddhist-leaning' people may be drawn instead to the secular mindfulness movement, where ideas and meditation practices are now far removed from their origins in traditional Buddhism. We are often told that meditation will calm us down, reduce our stress, help us develop concentration, reduce our blood pressure, lower our heart rate, aid our recovery from illness and help us ward off infections. And meditators are said to live longer! Such claims are difficult to verify – if we still feel stressed, perhaps we're not doing it right – and the tone is sometimes suspiciously similar to the blandishments of advertising.

This is not to deny the benefits of meditation, but if it has no wider context, we may be in the realm of a 'Buddhism-lite', a commodification of Buddhism as part of our consumer capitalism. We're invited to sign up for residential courses (sometimes in luxury locations), often advertised by attractive young women struggling with unfamiliar yoga poses. The number of courses offered suggests that not all mindfulness teachers have substantial personal experience. This can appear as the mass production and marketing of spiritual goods to make people feel better about themselves, rather than to help them behave more compassionately. And sometimes there are ulterior motives, such as reducing workplace stress to improve productivity, rather than to promote the personal well-being of staff.

Of course there are many experienced teachers with a long personal history of Buddhist practice. They may see the mindfulness movement as a new way to spread the Buddha's teaching in modern Western society, with the Asian religious elements removed. This could well appeal to 'secular Buddhists' who might be wary of anything which looks like a religious form of Buddhism. The problem with this 'meditation only' movement is that it plays into the Western obsession with *me* and *my* well-being, rather than exploring an ethical dimension which includes how we behave towards everyone else. In Western consumer societies this can amount almost to an idolatry of the self, where the individual's personal happiness is the most important objective, and is only achieved by *getting what we want*, whether from other people doing our bidding, or from the online catalogue. (These 'secular wellness' courses are sometimes offered at Buddhist centres, providing financial support for more spiritual activities – but perhaps at the same time diverting resources away from them.)

This reflects our Western obsession with the individual as more important than society as a whole, so that religion is often seen as a private matter rather than a communal activity. In the Buddha's time as well as our own, the process of urbanization risked the loss of a sense of community, with individuals feeling increasingly isolated. But the Buddha's teaching was concerned with the entire realm of sentient beings and their consciousness. In fact it was the inherent *selfishness* of this individualism which Buddhism sought to undermine, and an emphasis on community was there from the very beginning.

A practice completely free of ancient Asian influence would be unrecognisable as the Buddha's teaching. And a practice completely free of modern Western influence would be impossible, since that's the culture which surrounds us, whether we like it or not. The concentrated monastic-based Buddhism of traditional forms may be too rich for some of us to digest, while the diluted version of secular mindfulness may have almost lost the taste completely. I hesitate to suggest a form of 'Goldilocks Buddhism', where the porridge of practice is neither too hot or too cold but just right for us. That would avoid us having to make difficult changes about how we live our lives. But making such changes is often what a spiritual path is all about.

Can we find a middle way between an ancient religious Buddhism and the secularized quasi-Buddhism of the mindfulness industry? Something which is authentically Buddhist and authentically Western – whether we call it Buddhist practice or not? Maybe this search for authenticity is a fruitless quest. Even if we could find the elusive 'original Buddhism', it would be set in ancient India, and might be inappropriate in contemporary Western societies.

New Western Buddhisms

In both Europe and North America, there are new forms of what might be called 'Western Buddhism' which we could join, either in person or now via online 'cybersangha' forums. Usually run by lay people rather than monastics, they tend to be democratic and non-sectarian, with an open membership where supporters come and go. Teachings are often shared in discussion rather than given by a teacher, with an emphasis on informal guidelines, and meetings may have simple rituals or none. Examples of these new Buddhist sanghas include the Vipassana movement, Insight sanghas, and the Engaged Buddhism groups focusing on social justice rather than individual behaviour. Despite wide differences, a core of common practices includes meditation, ethical behaviour, developing loving-kindness, letting go of attachments, and seeking a path away from suffering and towards awakening.

The Buddhist traditions which developed in Asian countries – many miles apart and in different millennia – have all arrived in the West during the last few decades. For the first time we can draw on teachings and practices across the whole of Buddhism. This has led to suggestions of an *ecumenical* approach, including elements from the Theravada, Tibetan and Zen traditions – a process which could lead to confusion, because of the wide cultural differences between South-east Asia, Tibet and Japan. There is also the temptation to pick elements which appear attractive – the simplicity of Thai Theravada, the exotic Tibetan ritual, or the enigmatic poetry of Zen – and to ignore other teachings and practices which may make us feel uncomfortable, but whose challenges might be even more valuable for us.

Those dissatisfied with what they see as the dogmatic approach of an outdated Christianity may be attracted to Buddhism as a rational and atheistic philosophy, compatible with modern science and a more secular viewpoint. But this 'Buddhist modernism' tends to overlook the traditional elements of Buddhism which Westerners may find hard to accept, either because they seem so foreign to us (like karma and endless cycles of rebirth) or because they appear as simply irrelevant (like the cosmology of heaven and hell realms).

So there's an ongoing debate about which elements of teaching and practice should be retained by Western Buddhists, or taken up by those outside Buddhism who see the Buddha's teaching as potentially helpful in their spiritual lives. Most of us would agree there are some cultural elements which could safely be discarded. These are neatly hinted at by the title *You Don't Have to Sit on the Floor*, by Jim Pym (1941–2020), a Quaker and Pure Land Buddhist. But when Pym suggests that temples, bowing, chanting, ceremonial, scriptures and even meditation are *all* external forms which may be useful but are not necessary, we may begin to feel rather comfortable.[1] What is essential and what is peripheral? And how do we decide?

Buddhists wary of monastic authority often quote the Buddha's advice to the Kalamas, who were confused by visiting teachers denouncing each other's views. Who was telling the truth? The Buddha advised them not to rely on traditional teachings, scriptural authority, logic or inference, abstract analysis or speculation, or respect for a charismatic teacher. Instead they should abandon things they *know for themselves* are 'unwholesome ... blameworthy ... and censured by the wise', which bring only harm and suffering; and they should engage with things they *know for themselves* are 'wholesome, blameless, and praised by the wise', as these will bring benefit and happiness.[2] In other words, take responsibility for your own actions!

Religious and Secular Approaches

There's a growing distinction in the West between those we might call 'religious' Buddhists, focusing on traditional beliefs, and 'secular' Buddhists, looking for the forms of teaching and meditation most relevant in their everyday life. People sometimes use the words *secular* and *religious* as verbal rocks to throw at each other. Christians may decry the 'secular' as a rising tide of godless materialism, while humanists tend to see 'religious' people as pious or credulous. An aggressive secularism can be just as dogmatic as Christians who assert the literal truth of the Bible. It's easy to put on religious spectacles and see humanists as unbelievers, or to wear secular spectacles and dismiss religious people as gullible. But wearing these kinds of spectacles only serves to fuel our underlying prejudices.

When we call someone 'religious' we're describing either their *behaviour* – attending ceremonies or retreats, reading scriptures, meditating or praying – or their *attitudes*, which we may interpret as deeply sincere or insufferably pious. But there's also a sense in which 'religious' concerns are deeper and more abstract – the ways in which we relate to our human situation and face the prospect of death. Whenever we dismiss religious organizations as authoritarian and out-of-date, we may be overlooking their original purpose of helping people examine these deeper aspects of their life and its significance. An atheist philosopher or psychologist may consider the depths of the human psyche without following any religious *behaviour*, while a nominal churchgoer may have little concern for such self-examination.

I am reminded here of Trevor Ling, who apparently regarded the secular not as 'an alternative to religion, but as a set of clues to the nature of religion'.[3] We often interpret *secular* as 'worldly' or materialistic, but it can mean simply 'this-worldly', relating to the *present* world, the visible world we see around us, rather than any eternal or spiritual realm. So 'secular Buddhists' are concerned with *this* world in *this* time, paying more attention to the suffering of others and less to their own prospects of enlightenment. This seems to be in line with the Buddha's original teaching, showing concern for the welfare of all living beings, rather than focusing exclusively on the individual.

The more specific meaning of *religious* as 'belonging to a monastic order', and bound by its vows, contrasts with *secular* as being outside such orders. In this sense lay Buddhists are *secular* people, in contrast to *religious* monks and nuns, who are often seen as the experts, the 'full-time' Buddhists. But can a celibate monk or nun offer practical advice about sexual relationships, or problems between parents and children? To what extent can someone who lives in a *religious* monastic community offer guidance about how to live in the *secular* world of work and family life?

* * *

This is not a criticism of those who practise in monastic traditions. I will always be grateful to monks and nuns who have encouraged my own practice over many years, and to my Theravada and Zen lay friends. But many of us have more experience of living as lay Buddhists than someone who has spent their adult life in a monastery. We may look towards a different type of Buddhist practice, somewhere in between traditional 'religious' Buddhism and Stephen Batchelor's approach to secular dharma. One friend who describes himself as a 'secular Buddhist' is happy to discard any supernatural elements, while another is resistant to 'secular' as a term, and fascinated by the wealth and depth of religious narratives. But they are both regular meditators and spiritual teachers, and still have a great deal in common.

Even Stephen Batchelor's secular dharma does not abandon 'religious' Buddhism completely, since this might dilute the Buddha's teaching into a self-help manual for accepting our role in today's consumer society. After challenging traditional Buddhist teachings, the question he leaves hanging in the air is as relevant to Christians and humanists as it is to Western Buddhists: 'what would happen to a secular perspective inflected by the principles and values of the dharma?'[4]

Authority and Experience

If our contemporary practice needs to spring from compassionate behaviour, with an inner training of the heart and mind, relevant guidance may be more difficult to locate in traditions culturally far removed from us. Hierarchical organizations are sometimes more concerned with retaining their own authority than with enabling people to find a better way to live their lives. A misunderstanding in the 2003 film *Pirates of the Caribbean* illustrates these different approaches. Elizabeth Swann climbs aboard the *Black Pearl* and invokes the Pirate Code to negotiate safely with a temporary truce. She is surprised when Captain Barbossa imprisons her anyway, explaining with a leer that 'the Code is more what you call *guidelines* than actual *rules*'.

As a teenage Christian, I knew the rules of religion – the Ten Commandments, Jesus's instruction to love God and your neighbour. My obedience was at best patchy – I was particularly poor at honouring my mother and father – but at least I knew what the rules were. So when I became a Buddhist at university, the first thing was to learn the rules – the Four Noble Truths, the Five Precepts, and the Eightfold Path. Soon I could recite them if anyone asked me what Buddhists believed. Years later, I was shocked when a monk couldn't remember all the steps on the eightfold path. He didn't even know the rules! Eventually I realized that his ordinary daily practice – living the dharma rather than reading about it – was the *right effort* he had failed to recall.

Rules and guidelines are part of our everyday lives at home and at work. Those we meet as parents or children, teachers or students, colleagues or customers – may invoke rules to justify themselves, or explain why the rules don't apply to them. If I don't like a rule, it's only a guideline, but if you do something I don't like, you're breaking the rules! Some people find fixed rules stifling, while others are unsettled by the flexibility of guidelines.

As authority passed from the early Christian churches to later Orthodox and Catholic institutions, they became more authoritarian, imposing moral discipline and orthodox belief. This 'institutional Christianity' was challenged during the Reformation, when Protestant churches drew authority directly from the Bible in a more 'scriptural Christianity'. All Christians also rely on their personal experience to some extent; but this was sometimes seen as the primary inspiration, particularly within a mystical tradition we might call 'experiential Christianity'. Today we can still see both institutional Catholicism and Protestant scriptural fundamentalism, while Quakers and others continue to rely more heavily on personal experience.

Buddhism has seen a somewhat similar pattern. Those who take the Pali Canon as the authentic words of the Buddha, or who see the Mahayana *Heart Sutra* as the ultimate revelation of truth, are supporting a kind of 'scriptural Buddhism'. Those who treat monks (and less often nuns) with great reverence, as authority figures who perform rituals on behalf of the community, could be seen as part of an 'institutional Buddhism'. All Buddhists again rely on their personal experience, but Westerners in particular tend to see this as the guiding authority in their practice of meditation and ethical behaviour, in a form of 'experiential Buddhism'.

Hierarchy and Democracy

At the beginning of the *Mahaparinibbana Sutta* the Buddha warns the king of Magadha against attacking the Vajjians. They are said to hold frequent peaceful meetings, to respect their constitution and traditions, their elders and ethical code, and to welcome teachers from elsewhere – and thus they 'may be expected to prosper and not decline'.[5] These were the values which guided the early monastic sanghas, set up on a more or less democratic basis, without centralized power or authoritative abbots. Unlike modern democracies, they relied on unanimous agreement rather than majority opinion. With a willingness to set up new groups rather than suppress dissident views as heretical, Buddhism has generally seen fewer warring factions than some other religious traditions.

But after the Buddha's death, monastic organizations gradually became more hierarchical, developing a more authoritative (and sometimes more authoritarian) attitude which eventually tended to become the norm. Buddhism has often been allied to state patronage in Asian societies, as Christian churches have been in Europe. Civic authorities prefer dealing with a single religious institution, applying one set of rules and teachings, which helps to unify a diverse population. This allows the religion to prosper, often financially as well as spiritually, but at the expense of becoming the status quo which must be maintained. This often makes for hierarchical structures and an inability to change.

In the West, Buddhism is free of such patronage, with organizations funded by their members and supporters. This may possibly allow monastic sanghas to become gradually less hierarchical and more democratic. Western Buddhists are usually not interested in supporting a monastic sangha to gain merit for a favourable rebirth, and expect to be regarded as equal members rather than supporters or second-class Buddhists.

We accept hierarchies at work and in the armed forces and government, but most voluntary groups are often run on more democratic lines, apart from those such as the Freemasons and the Scout movement – and of course religious organizations. Christians accept the authority of a hierarchical clergy, because of the power invested in them by their Catholic or Protestant churches, often claiming an 'apostolic succession' from the early disciples.

The equivalent in traditional Buddhism is a 'dharma transmission', in which senior teachers bring a new teacher into a lineage traced back to the Buddha himself. Although the Buddha ruled out any leadership succession, telling the monks to take the dharma as their guide after his death, the bossy monk Kassapa attempted to assume this role. He is seen as the founder of the Zen tradition, which began when the Buddha silently held up a flower on Vulture Peak and only Kassapa received this direct 'mind-to-mind transmission'. But this story is a later addition absent from early texts, and the lineage lists include legendary as well as historical figures.

Buddhist monastics and Christian clergy could claim authority when they alone had access to the scriptures, but as literacy advanced, this exclusivity was undermined. Buddhist teachers are now respected instead for their long practice of the dharma, and their ability to communicate with fellow practitioners. This will hopefully allow sanghas to be organized on more democratic lines, like most other voluntary bodies. Stephen Batchelor envisages a community where members offer each other mutual support in their spiritual development, each treating the others as equals and respecting their understanding and experience.[6]

The model of spiritual master and pupil makes me feel uncomfortable. Spiritual friends have often offered me wise and compassionate support, particularly at times of crisis or despair. But the advice given by senior monks has sometimes felt obtrusive, inviting me to conform rather than addressing questions with an open heart. When I once expressed a lack of connection with monastic ritual, for example, I was firmly told: 'You need to learn to be a *follower*, Robert.' This conversation had obviously begun with different assumptions about authority! Whether or not we call this 'institutional Buddhism', there was something here I found profoundly saddening, and it prompted me to change course.

Who Says So?

When the Buddha tells the Kalamas not to rely on scripture or tradition or reasoning or a charismatic teacher, he is not merely listing unreliable ways of looking for truth. He is gently leading them away from the search for abstract truth or doctrine, and recommending instead a path of *action*. He helps the Kalamas to see that actions influenced by greed, hatred and delusion will lead to their harm and sorrow, while actions free from these poisons will bring them benefit and happiness. But we're still left to ponder exactly *which* things are censured by the wise and which things are praised by them. And who exactly *are* these wise people, who seem to know everything about wholesome and unwholesome actions?

Western Buddhists who are hostile to their Christian cultural background may be tempted to regard 'scriptural Buddhism' and 'institutional Buddhism' as irrelevant. Both early Theravada and later Mahayana scriptures often include supernatural and magical stories, which surely can't be true. Theravada, Tibetan and Zen monasteries have long been patriarchal hierarchies, and this approach seems inappropriate in modern Western culture. Would we not do much better to opt instead for an 'experiential Buddhism' based solely on our own personal experience?

This would surely be a mistake. While Buddhist scriptures include many mythical as well as historical elements, they're our primary source for the Buddha's teachings. Buddhist monastic institutions may be hierarchical and authoritarian, but they've also nurtured many dedicated and experienced teachers, whose development and explanation of the original teachings has been invaluable. Monasteries and scriptures have preserved the Buddha's teachings and brought them down to us. Without the Pali canon and the monastic sangha, there would be no Buddhism today. They deserve our gratitude and respect, even if we can't always agree with them, and they seem to be imposing irrelevant rules. Setting aside our own habitual reactions to hierarchy and authority, we might be able to see monastics instead as the parents and guardians of the awkward teenagers we call Western Buddhists.

The cult of the individual is now a dominant force in Western consumerism. We're always being told we need faster cars and more hamburgers. We know that resources are finite, and that our current pattern of activity threatens the planet's future. But we often want *more for ourselves*, even if this means giving less to everyone else. This is an example of how our greed, hate and delusion gets in the way of clear thinking. Our personal experience – or rather our habitual *interpretation* of our experience – is far from infallible. How wise is it to reach for that second helping or another glass of wine? Did that person mean to be rude, or are we being paranoid? Are we really tired this morning, or just too lazy to get out of bed? If we can't trust our own judgement in such minor examples – and our inability to resist the lure of consumerism – how can we rely on our personal authority to guide our spiritual life?

Perhaps we need all three areas of authority to guide our practice. But like the Kalamas, we need to *choose for ourselves* how we relate to them, rather than have those choices made for us, either by an unquestioning devotion to the Pali texts as the word of the Buddha, or by monastic teachers telling us not to choose anything outside the status quo. Having said that, if the Buddha is our true teacher, we need to listen respectfully to what he has to say. If the dharma is the medicine for all suffering, we need to find skilful ways of accessing and understanding this teaching. And if the sangha are indeed the wise and compassionate, we need to listen to them as well – whether or not they are monastics.

The Wisdom of the Elders

There's also an important *fourth* authority – those whom the Buddha calls 'the wise'. In pre-industrial China and Japan, those who only behave well because of the power of the law are seen as foolish and inferior. Those 'elders' regarded as 'the wise' are those whose moral conduct is *naturally* blameless. This is very different in modern Western society! Who are the wise? We meet people whose spiritual practice is longer and deeper than ours, and who can be relied on for sound advice. They may be dharma teachers, monastics, or spiritual friends in our local Zen group. Sometimes we can even be our own wise spiritual friend. And 'the wise' don't have to be Buddhists. Who taught me about right and wrong, before I learned any church rules? Who showed me years of generosity, loving-kindness and understanding, before I had even heard of Buddhism? The wise are everywhere, if we have the patience to listen, and the willingness to accept their advice with gratitude.

Before we get carried away with exciting changes in Western Buddhism, and the possibilities they suggest, we should remember that most traditional Buddhist organizations are inherently conservative. The Theravada Forest Sangha cannot offer full ordination to women, as this would sever the link with a more patriarchal Buddhism in Thailand. The efforts of Western Tibetan Buddhist centres to conserve and protect Tibetan culture limits their scope for innovation. Zen centres in America and Britain often have a hierarchy of monastic ranks, and extremely detailed rules about how to behave, from the meditation hall to the bathroom.

* * *

At the end of his *Buddhism from Within*, Daizui MacPhillamy (1945-2003), head of the Soto Zen Order of Buddhist Contemplatives, encourages potential Buddhists to find a tradition which suits them and stay put. Wandering from one teacher to another, people may pick and choose only what attracts them, leaving out elements they find difficult. The different Buddhist traditions have developed over centuries or even millennia, distilling the wisdom of generations of those seeking the truth. So, he asks, why would we ignore their kind offers of assistance 'and insist upon "re-inventing the wheel" by creating a new form of practice?'[7]

I think there are three answers to Daizui's rhetorical question. First, he argues here that we *should* rely on tradition, but as he points out earlier in *Buddhism from Within*, the Buddha specifically advised the Kalamas *not* to rely on tradition. Second, Buddhism has flourished in each new culture only by changing and adapting to each new context. If Chinese and Tibetan and Japanese followers of the Buddha had been content to copy the tradition they inherited, the dharma could hardly have taken root in their countries. If we simply follow tradition now, there can be no genuinely Western Buddhism. Third, for the first time in history, all the main Buddhist traditions can be seen together in the same place. Instead of choosing Theravada or Tibetan or Zen, and expecting it to remain the same as its Asian form, we have a unique opportunity to draw wisely on the riches of all these traditions to find what works for us as Western Buddhists. This is not so much ignoring their wisdom as building upon it.

The tricky question of what to take from Asian Buddhism and what to discard is answered most imaginatively by Maezumi Roshi (1931-95), one of the Japanese masters who brought Zen to the West. He used to tell his students, 'Taste as much of this as you can. Swallow what you need and spit out the rest.'[8] But it is very difficult to distinguish honestly and imaginatively between what we *need* and what we merely *like*. We must be careful to spit out only what is superfluous, swallowing and digesting everything genuinely nutritious – even if the taste is bitter at first.

Chapter 3

Finding a Local Path

Having looked for a middle way between Asian and Western, religious and secular, and authority and experience, how might we apply this in our own practice? For unofficial Buddhists, deciding what to retain and what to discard is a personal decision, even if it is informed by reading the scriptures, visiting Buddhist centres and listening to the wise. The answers may be different depending on where we live, as every European and English-speaking country has its own unique cultural background. Since Buddhism has changed in spreading from India to China, Japan and Tibet – and to other Asian countries – we should not be surprised if it takes a variety of forms in different parts of the West.

So those of us in the UK may begin to ask ourselves what a 'British Buddhism' might eventually look like, and meanwhile how should we practise as British Buddhists? Whether you are reading this in Europe or North America – or anywhere else – the question is the same. How should we practise in our own cultural setting, and what might a Western Buddhism look like in our neck of the woods, or our part of the urban jungle?

Theravada, Zen – and What Then?

I was not always an unofficial Buddhist. At university my teenage Christian faith gave way to searching for a different spiritual path. One of my tutors was Professor Trevor Ling, and I attended his lectures on world religions, scribbling notes furiously. But when he finished the story of the Buddha's life and teaching, there was just a blank sheet of paper in front of me. The narrative had bypassed my intellectual curiosity and entered my heart. Without realizing it, I had become a Buddhist.

People may change when their minds have been opened or when their hearts have been broken. What I thought of as a search for enlightenment was probably more an attempt to escape from grief. My father had died suddenly, and the lecture on the Buddha came at exactly the right moment. So I read Walpola Rahula's *What the Buddha Taught* and started trying to meditate. For many years I practised as a Theravada Buddhist, attending retreats at Forest Sangha monasteries. But I began gradually to feel uncomfortable with a tradition where laypeople were 'supporters' rather than members. The Buddha spoke of a *fourfold* sangha – monks and nuns, laymen and laywomen – but the Forest Sangha had a hierarchy where lay people were clearly expected not to question monastic decisions. This ancient Asian model felt less appropriate in modern Britain, at least for me.

While teaching world religions for the Open University, I began a research project to see how Buddhist traditions were adapting in their British context. Visiting monasteries, centres and local groups, I interviewed leaders and members in Theravada, Tibetan and Zen groups, as well as new Buddhist movements, and spent time on retreat with them. My doctoral thesis became a book called *British Buddhism* – a slightly misleading title, since it covered a wide variety of Buddhists in Britain, from Asian communities to Western groups.

Meanwhile, friends began to visit a local Zen monastery, and soon I went with them, visiting regularly for meditation, retreats and festivals, in a less austere atmosphere. This was my spiritual home for most of the next twenty years, impressed by the teaching that men and women, monastics and lay people, all practised as equals. But I felt increasingly detached from the elaborate monastic ceremonial, the processions and incense and chanting. This seemed to echo Christian ritual, and the Zen liturgy was written in the seventeenth-century language of the King James Bible and the Book of Common Prayer, rarely used now in the Church of England or anywhere else. This language and ritual were also used in lay groups, reinforced by visiting monks and nuns, and any resistance was met with the assertion that you mustn't pick and choose. But as a lay Buddhist, why would I wish to engage with monastic ritual? There was also a hierarchical 'seven ranks of the priesthood', and a lineage of dharma transmission referred to as 'apostolic succession' from the Buddha to the present monastic leaders.

I was happy with Zen practice, but not with ceremonial, lineage and dharma transmission within a hierarchy. A monastic-based practice was simply not for me. I was reminded of a Theravada monk who disrobed after many years, saying he felt the shoe was too tight – not criticizing the tradition, but finding it too cramped for him. I can't see myself any more as a 'lay' Buddhist, but simply as someone who wishes to follow the Buddha's dharma in contemporary Britain.

If we follow a Theravada, Tibetan or Zen tradition, we're practising a form of Asian Buddhism from Thailand or Tibet or Japan. We're really Buddhists in Britain or Buddhists in America, rather than British Buddhists or American Buddhists. Many of us, particularly convert Buddhists with no Asian ethnic background, are not committed to a specific tradition, and may be looking for something which Asian forms cannot provide for Westerners. The American Zen teacher and poet Norman Fischer (b. 1946) suggests that these unaffiliated practitioners may be 'Buddhist pioneers', rather than people who can't choose which monastery to visit.[1]

Maybe we should listen to the words attributed to Gandhi (1869–1948): 'Be the change that you wish to see'. Our practice has to find an accommodation, a balance, a merger if you like, between the original teaching of the Buddha, the various subsequent Buddhist traditions, and our own background – the cultural and spiritual identity of our own country. Choosing what works well in different traditions and bringing new elements together seems a wise course to take, though it may not be easy, and guidance may be hard to come by. Buddhist monastics can really only invite us to join their tradition or try another one. If you suggest a different approach, you're likely to be put firmly in your place as a lay person, or invited to leave.

Buddhist practice begins from where we are now, in terms of our culture, lifestyle, level of commitment and tradition. For what it's worth, I'm a retired middle-class white British man, living for many years with my wife, and practising Buddhism since I was a student. (Your own answer to this question may be much more interesting than mine!) I'm drawn to Zen practice, which I understand as regular meditation, engaging with the Zen precepts, and developing compassion for others. But I've also been influenced by the secular Buddhism of Stephen and Martine Batchelor. My commitment is less than perfect, but my spiritual practice is a central part of my life rather than an interesting hobby. So how should I practise as a somewhat secular British Zen person, who's fairly serious about all this?

If we're looking for a Buddhist practice which reflects our own customs and values, as well as retaining the Buddha's original teachings, what would such a practice look like? How can the Four Noble Truths and the eightfold path be expressed in a contemporary context, as practical tasks to be engaged with, rather than a list of things Buddhists believe?

Buddhism in Britain

As an example we might look at Buddhism in Britain, now on a par with Judaism as the fourth largest religion in the country, after Christianity, Islam and Hinduism. The earliest Buddhists here were all laymen (and a very few laywomen), but a monastic sangha was always seen as essential for the dharma to flourish. A century later, there are now traditional Theravada, Tibetan and Zen monastic sanghas, each with their lay members or supporters. It is still often assumed that ordination is the mark of the committed Buddhist, even within a Westernised organization such as Triratna (formerly the Western Buddhist Order). The conclusion to *British Buddhism* explains how these different traditions often have similar features, such as: largely traditional silent meditation; devotional activities and teachings; a programme of retreats and courses; some emphasis on textual study; a common ethical code for all members; a significant teacher–student element, usually with Western teachers; and increased lay participation.[2] Could one of these organizations expand in popularity and become the predominant British Buddhism?

This seems unlikely. The hierarchy of Theravada, Tibetan and Zen monastic organizations – each with their monastic ritual, and their Pali, Tibetan or Japanese chanting – can all sometimes feel out of touch in a democratic English-speaking country. Four more recent organizations – the Order of Buddhist Contemplatives, the Community of Interbeing, the New Kadampa Tradition and the Triratna Buddhist Community – are still centred on an ordained hierarchy, and each was created by an individual monastic, with their own personal interpretation of the organization's Asian roots. Although Soka Gakkai and the Samatha Trust are both wholly lay movements, they are also unlikely to expand into a dominate British Buddhism. Soka Gakkai members chant in Sino-Japanese, as part of a global movement with Japanese leaders; and the Samatha Trust is firmly within the Theravada tradition, retaining some of the elements of Thai monasticism.

It's not unusual for traditions to retain links with their Asian parent organizations, to chant in Asian languages, or to be brought to the West by a single monk or nun. All these elements are wholly legitimate – but they have their own characteristics, which are unlikely to lead to a British Buddhism. Moreover, traditional monastic Buddhist schools tend to view authority as resting in their texts, lineage and current teachers, while Western convert Buddhists are more likely to place greater weight on their own experience. It is difficult to see how the authority of texts, lineage or teachers can inform a new British Buddhism in the same way as they contribute to the Theravada, Tibetan or Zen traditions.

Some Western Buddhists do find a heart connection with the simple beauty of Thai Buddhist iconography, the rich symbolism of Tibetan practice, or the Japanese flavour of a Zen monastery. But for more unofficial Buddhists, these elements may feel like slightly exotic Asian imports, rather like growing plants from a different continent instead of native species. The hierarchical structures, monastic ritual and foreign languages can somehow seem to get in the way, forming a distraction rather than a support for the practice of awakening the compassionate heart.

There has always been a strand of independent lay dharma practice in Britain. As early as 1909 the Buddhist Society proposed 'a lay brotherhood and sisterhood', bound together by 'the purity of a selfless interest' in the Buddha's teaching, rather than monastic vows.[3] Sixty years later the society's formidable president, the barrister and prolific author Christmas Humphreys (1901–83), described most English Buddhists as 'frankly eclectic', seeking out whatever would best support their spiritual journey. He looked forward to a new form of Buddhism which could evolve naturally, as traditional forms had done, and which would gradually 'blend with the best of Western science, psychology and social science' and so become part of Western culture.[4]

As well as about thirty different Theravada, Tibetan, Zen and other groups in Britain, each with a few hundred or a few thousand followers, there are many unaffiliated Buddhists, often uncomfortable with existing traditions, which they see as closely related to Asian Buddhism. Practising on their own or in small groups, this is almost certainly the largest category of convert Buddhists in Britain, though they can hardly be called a group as a whole – many of them are only aware of a few others who are of the same mind as they are.

Any new form of Western Buddhism which developed would probably be a democratic and collaborative venture, rather than the work of a single charismatic leader. When an individual imports or adapts an Asian tradition, their personal experience will colour whatever emerges, with somewhat idiosyncratic results. For example, the Zen practice in the Order of Buddhist Contemplatives strongly reflects the background of the founder, Roshi Kennett (1924-96), an Englishwoman brought up in Anglicanism, and so has a different character from Zen practice in Japan, or in other Western Zen groups. And the combination of Theravada and Tibetan teaching and practice in the Western Buddhist Order (now Triratna), founded by Sangharakshita (1925-2018) and based on his travels in India, is far removed from both traditional schools. It may not always be clear to followers of these traditions that their founders have made significant choices about what to include or exclude or change. (This lack of awareness can also be seen in other organizations. One of my Soka Gakkai interviewees had practised for twelve years, but did not recognize the term Theravada Buddhism. Even the staunchest Protestants and Catholics have at least heard of each other!)

Principles for the Future?

So how might Buddhism develop in Britain or America or other Western countries? Which teachings and practices would be emphasized, and how might they differ from more traditional forms? Which scriptures would be seen as central or peripheral? Which ancient or contemporary narratives of leading figures would be emphasized? How would the personal experience of practice be viewed, and how might the development of wisdom and compassion be promoted? Which ethical precepts might be adopted, and how would practitioners be encouraged to engage with them? How might new practice groups be organized, and how would they and their leaders relate to society as a whole? Would they appeal mainly to those who (like me) might be seen as 'posh white Buddhists', or more broadly to people of all social and ethnic backgrounds?

The honest answer to all these questions is the same: we don't know, and it's too early to tell. The Buddha's guidance to the Kalamas helpfully suggests that we shouldn't rely on tradition or scripture or abstract reasoning or a charismatic teacher. But we still need to work out for ourselves who 'the wise' are, which things they approve or disapprove of, and how we might move from ethical behaviour towards the transformative development of loving-kindness and compassion. So any predictions are tentative and speculative – but let's gaze into the crystal ball anyway.

There are perhaps four underlying principles which might support potential Western forms of Buddhism, again using Britain as an example. First, a new 'ecumenical' form of teaching and practice could draw on elements from all three main Buddhist traditions – Theravada, Tibetan and Zen – while discarding elements from the indigenous cultures of ancient India or modern Thailand, pre-Buddhist Tibet or medieval Japan. This is a notoriously difficult process. If we merely choose what appeals from each tradition, we risk losing those more challenging elements which could be essential for our practice. If we restrict ourselves to elements found in all three traditions, we may be left with a residual or basic Buddhism with no flavour of its own, rather than the genuine taste of the dharma. Nevertheless this process must be undertaken, if only by trial and error, to see what works for us in our own culture, what makes that heart connection and enables us to develop our compassionate behaviour towards others. We're not Thai or Tibetan or Japanese – so we have no need to practise as if we were.

Second, a genuinely British Buddhism – or any genuinely Western Buddhism – will be practised wholly in the vernacular, like the Buddhism of ancient India, Tibet and Japan. Many Buddhists with an Asian background love to chant in their own language, reminding them of their cultural roots; and some convert Buddhists also feel that chanting in Pali or Tibetan or Japanese makes an important emotional connection with the source of the tradition. But the Buddha seems to have taken a different view. In the *Aranavibhanga Sutta* he explains to the monks that when teaching the dharma 'one should not override normal usage'.[5] When two monks suggested putting the teaching into classical Sanskrit verse, to prevent monks from different areas teaching in different dialects, the Buddha firmly scolded them, insisting that his teaching should be taught and learned 'each in his own dialect'.[6] Surely we should follow this clear advice. Readings, teachings and discussion, and any liturgy which might be needed, will all be in contemporary English (or in other European languages) rather than chanting in Pali or Sanskrit, Tibetan or Japanese. A very few untranslatable terms will remain – such as buddha, dharma and sangha – but even these are passing into common usage, and included in English dictionaries. No truly Western Buddhism can rely on Asian languages.

Third – and most controversial – is the need to reflect the increasingly egalitarian and democratic culture of modern Western countries, by abandoning the traditional pattern of a hierarchical and conservative monastic core supported by lay people. This is happening in various Western Buddhist groups, particularly in North America, with people defining themselves by their commitment to dharma practice, rather than a lay or monastic identity. Members are encouraged to feel a stronger connection with their sangha, if they are helping to contribute to its running themselves. In our local informal Zen group, for example, we take turns to bring a short reading and to lead the discussion after meditation, to make sure that we share the responsibility between us.

Fourth, a Western Buddhism will need to draw imaginatively on elements of *Western* culture, as has happened in the previous cultures where Buddhism has taken root. In Britain, for example, the Church of England has been the dominant religious tradition since the Reformation, independent from Roman Catholicism, with a liturgy in contemporary language rather than in Latin or Elizabethan English. Although it retains an ecclesiastical hierarchy, there is improved (though sadly not yet complete) gender equality. It could be seen as a non-dogmatic, all-inclusive broad church, rather than a narrow sect with rigid rules and doctrines. Despite falling attendance, it can still foster a genuine sense of community in local areas. There are also interesting echoes of English seasonal traditions, with winter/Christmas, spring/Easter, and summer/harvest festivals.

Can we see forms of Western Buddhism which could follow these four principles? They might include elements from Theravada, Tibetan and Zen teaching and practice, translated into modern English or other European languages, with an ecumenical rather than exclusive approach. They would hopefully be democratic spiritual communities with complete gender equality, not relying on either a monastic core or Asian Buddhist organizations. Perhaps there could even be seasonal festivals celebrating the life and teaching of the Buddha – though this might be too much for the secular Buddhists! Again the emphasis would need to be on what works for the people involved, what enables their practice to develop, to awaken the compassionate heart.

Buddhists and Christians

If modern Western society has invented its own religion, it is surely the cult of the individual. Religion is often seen as the personal interest of the minority, rather than the central concern of the community as a whole. Religious organizations – including Christian churches and Buddhist monastic traditions – have sometimes show a marked reluctance to engage with social and political issues. Although the USA and Britain are among the world's most unequal nations, in terms of the gap between the rich and the poor, Christians and Buddhists have not always been at the forefront of campaigns to eliminate poverty, or to combat gender bias, racial discrimination, environmental destruction or climate change. There are notable exceptions in both traditions. Those in and around Buddhism include the Zen Peacemakers, the Order of Interbeing, the Network of Engaged Buddhists, the Free Tibet movement, and activities ranging from environmental activism to psychotherapeutic initiatives and prison chaplaincy work. Hopefully emerging forms of Buddhism can draw on these examples, encouraging practitioners to see themselves as part of their local, regional, national and international communities. Christians and Buddhists would do well to encourage each other here.

The ancient Christian practice of *tithing* – giving one-tenth of your earnings to support the church – might be adapted by Buddhists, not to sustain temples or monasteries, but to help the wider community. If Buddhists regularly donated a proportion of their income to local, national and international charities, this would both support those who are suffering and help to protect our environment. Christians can also offer Buddhists an example of *enculturation* – the process of becoming normalized in a particular society. When the Christian church arrived in a pagan Britain, it must have appeared as an alien culture. Now it is so much a feature of Britishness that the Church of England has long been described (somewhat unfairly) as the Conservative Party at prayer. This lengthy enculturation process, through which a completely foreign religion emerged as the established church, surely has something to teach us, as unofficial Buddhists attempt to find common ground between the Buddha's teaching and our cultural background. Let's hope it doesn't take quite as long.

In return Buddhists may have something important to offer their Christian friends. The practice of meditation doesn't have to be linked to Buddhist teaching, and can be beneficial to those of all religions or none. It might even help Christians rediscover their own medieval meditation tradition. Buddhism could also offer a challenging ethical practice. As we shall see in later chapters, engaging with the Buddhist precepts involves not only avoiding a list of harmful actions, but also developing a wide range of positive qualities, from loving-kindness and generosity to truthfulness and insight. This encourages Buddhists and Christians alike to lead ethical lives not from fear of punishment or a sense of obligation, but rather from a wish to benefit themselves and each other – and hopefully all living beings.

Gazing into the future, we may catch a glimpse of new possibilities. At one end of the spectrum, a single organization could become the dominant form of Buddhism in Britain or North America or other Western countries. This might be either a Theravada, Tibetan or Zen tradition, if the others gradually faded, or it might be a new and as yet unknown Western form of dharma practice. The history of a fragmented Christian denominationalism suggests this might not be the case for a very long time. At the other end, official and unofficial Buddhists may continue to practise in many different ways. It remains to be seen whether we end up with a single Buddhist organization (either an old one or a new one) or a thousand flowers blooming independently of each other – or something in between.

Our local 'unofficial' group has met each month for several years now, for meditation and discussion – a group of spiritual friends rather than anything more formal. The group includes committed Theravada and Zen practitioners, meditators sympathetic to Buddhism, and one or two secular Buddhists. Some of us have been on retreats and courses at nearby Theravada and Zen monasteries, or at Samye Ling Tibetan Buddhist Centre, not far away in the Scottish borders. We have even had one or two of our Christian friends come and meditate with us.

Chapter 4

Towards a Zen Path?

If we're looking for a form of spiritual practice for unofficial Buddhists – including Buddhist-leaning outsiders as well as free-range, secular or not-just Buddhists – where would such a path begin? How might it relate to the existing traditions of Buddhism? Could it draw on one or more of them, or perhaps reject them all in favour of something new?

All three main traditions have what might be seen as a conservative monastic hierarchy, with different links to their Asian cultural background. South-east Asian immigrant communities often wish to retain traditional forms of Theravada Buddhism in the Western countries where they now live. Tibetan Buddhists – whether ethnic Tibetans or Western converts – are keen to preserve the culture now exiled from Tibet itself, with the hope of an eventual return. Although Zen has strong cultural links to Japan, some Western Zen groups have moved away from the traditional pattern, and there are even Christian priests who are also recognized as Zen teachers. If Zen can be practised by Christians as well as Buddhists, this suggests it has real potential for our unofficial path.

There has been much fruitless discussion about whether Zen is really a religion at all. Trevor Ling suggests that Buddhism *itself* was not originally a religion, at least not in the sense of a system of individual salvation. The Buddha's teaching was concerned with 'the whole realm of sentient being', rather than only our personal destiny. But it grew into a more theistic belief and practice, with devotion paid to the Buddha's supposed supernatural qualities and miraculous powers. As its original rational spirit was gradually lost, Buddhism became what Ling calls 'a merely religious organization', rather than a more radical 'ideology for the restructuring of human nature and society'.[1] Those who see Buddhism as primarily about the individual's enlightenment might read the *Sigalaka Sutta*, where the Buddha explains in detail how children and parents, students and teachers, husbands and wives, employers and workers – as well as householders and monastics – should behave towards one another.[2] He is clearly interested in these important social relationships as part of the spiritual development of the community as a whole.

Zen Comes West

The American Zen teacher Norman Fischer describes the Japanese pioneers who brought Zen to the West as 'renegades and visionaries in their own culture', who were hoping to escape from the formality of Zen in Japan, which was 'encrusted with tradition and conventionality'.[3] The first of these pioneers was the celebrated Buddhist scholar and practitioner D.T. Suzuki (1870–1966), who contrasted the complex metaphysics of other Buddhist traditions with Zen's simplicity and pragmatism, where teachings emerge from our own experience rather than from dogma or scriptures. He argues that with no deity or ceremonial rites, and no realm beyond death, Zen rejects external authority and emphasizes the 'inner purity and goodness' of human beings. Suzuki confirms that Christians can practice Zen as well as Buddhists, like large and small fish 'both contentedly living in the same ocean'. But he adds: 'Zen is the ocean, Zen is the air, Zen is the mountain, Zen is thunder and lightning, the spring flower, summer heat, and winter snow.'[4] For readers who find this suddenly confusing – welcome to Zen!

His namesake Shunryu Suzuki Roshi (1904–71) has been called a 'founding father' of Zen in America, partly due to his 1970 *Zen Mind, Beginner's Mind* – perhaps the most widely read book on Zen in English. The opening statement probably horrified learned teachers in Japan: 'In the beginner's mind there are many possibilities, but in the expert's there are few.'[5] Suzuki Roshi told his students it did not matter if they believed in another religion, as Zen practice 'has nothing to do with some particular religious belief ... Our practice is for everyone.'[6] He also told them they were neither priests nor lay people, and in the 1960s freewheeling culture he and other teachers did not focus too much on following the Zen precepts. Suzuki Roshi encouraged a careful but spontaneous approach, meeting each situation as it comes, rather than trying to work everything out in advance. He once told his students, 'Zen is to feel your way along in the dark, not knowing what you will meet, not already knowing what to do.'[7]

We have already seen that Taizan Maezumi Roshi invited his Western students to taste all of Zen and spit out what they could not swallow. 'Find your own way', he told them. Again this would not please traditional Zen teachers in Japan. But Maezumi also insisted on the value of ceremonial, and the patriarchal lineage of Zen Buddhism. This traditional approach is also seen from Westerners who trained in Japan and followed the conventions which the 'renegades and visionaries' wished to escape from. In *Three Pillars of Zen* (1965), and later in *Zen: Dawn in the West* (1979), the American Zen teacher Philip Kapleau (1912–2004) is clear that Zen is a religion with ritual and devotional practice at its heart. Chanting, bowing, prostrations, offerings and 'regular confession and repentance ceremonies' are inseparable from meditation practice, as they 'refine the emotions and purify the mind', reducing the ego and helping 'to liberate our inherent compassion'. (It's worth noting here that the Buddha identified attachment to rites and rituals as a fetter to be abandoned.) Kapleau describes prayer as 'the lifeblood of religion', and claims that Avalokiteshvara, the bodhisattva of compassion, 'never fails to respond to impassioned cries for help from those who believe in him'. (This sounds rather more like Catholicism than the Buddha's teaching to me.) He concludes that in adapting Zen for the West, his Japanese training will prevent him 'throwing out the baby with the bathwater', but he may well have kept them both.[8]

D.T. Suzuki's influence was also felt in Britain. Christmas Humphreys' popular *Buddhism* (1951), describes Zen as the apex of Buddhism, no longer needing to rely on any scriptures, rituals, incense, chanting or monastic robes.[9] Yet all these features are still present in Western Zen today, complete with prominent Zen masters and a monastic core. Both masters and monasteries are imaginatively sidestepped by W.J. Gabb in *The Goose is Out* (1956), where he suggests a more secular approach, living in 'a Zen monastery which I call the world', and where the other monks are simply the people around him. The presiding master of this 'community of mankind' sets repeated problems to solve, but has also been like a mother to him: 'As for me, I know him quite simply as my life.'[10]

Roshi Kennett argues in her provocatively titled *Zen Is Eternal Life* (1976) that Zen can only be understood 'using the heart of faith' rather than rationally, so that 'Zen is an intuitive RELIGION and not a philosophy or way of life.'[11] She later asserts that Zen is *not* atheistic, since the Buddha found 'an Unborn, Undying, Unchanging, Uncreated', which 'gave Him His enlightenment', and which is the same as what Christians call God.[12]

Almost all Buddhists would beg to differ here. What the Buddha found is better translated as *'freedom* from birth', *'freedom* from death', rather than a state that is unborn and undying. (There are no capital letters in Pali – and capitalized personal pronouns for the Buddha make him sound like a saviour rather than a teacher.)

Kennett's successor as head of the Order of Buddhist Contemplatives, Daizui MacPhillamy, glosses over her theistic claims, arguing that Zen can be seen as 'an almost secular philosophy' or alternatively as 'a deeply religious practice involving faith, ceremony, precepts, and spiritual intuition'.[13] He admits in *Buddhism from Within* that this is an unusual religion with neither soul nor sin nor afterlife – though Buddhist teachers may use terms like 'the Eternal' or 'God', which assumes the existence of some 'ultimate reality'. (Again the Buddha used no such terms.) Daizui argues that ceremonies may be helpful, but are not strictly necessary. For some, ceremonial 'can be a doorway into experiencing Buddhist teachings in a way which words simply cannot convey', but for others it 'fails to communicate what is intended', and they see little point in it.[14]

The Practice of Zen

During my first Zen retreat, over twenty years ago now, the senior monk asked each newcomer privately how things were going. I said everything was fine apart from the dreary chanting, which sounded like singing psalms in church. Smiling, he said this was *aversion*, and offered me three choices. Campaign for them to change the music – very small chance of success. Go away and not come back again – that would be a pity. 'Or you can change your mind!' He looked me in the eye, and I saw this wasn't about the chanting, or about altering your opinions. *Change your mind.* Maybe that's what Buddhism is all about.

Norman Fischer's *What is Zen?* (2016) has been most helpful here, though I can't always agree with his answers to the probing questions from co-author Susan Moon. He describes Zen Buddhism as 'an Asian religion now practiced all over the world', with the 'clergy, ritual, scripture, hierarchy' common to all religions. As well as meditation, Zen practice includes 'retreats, talks, ceremonies, meetings with teachers, textual study'.[15] However, the object is not to achieve some personal goal, but to let go of this self-centred approach, so that we can become progressively liberated from the habitual views and behaviour which restricts our happiness.

Zen is a bit like learning to swim or riding a bicycle. Instructions can tell you how to move your arms and legs, but cannot convey the sense of gliding through the water, or sweeping effortlessly downhill. Similarly, Zen writers try to use words to describe something beyond words. This brings us to Dogen (1200–53), the Japanese monk who founded the Soto Zen school at the Eihei-ji Temple, east of Fukui, after his return from his training in China. He had wrestled with the contrast between the innate wisdom of all beings – often referred to as 'Buddha-nature' – and the energetic and persistent practice of all the great teachers. So his meditation guidance begins with some challenging questions: 'The complete way flows everywhere: what use is practice and awakening? The essential teaching is freely available: how could effort be needed? The dharma is always right where you are: why wander off to search for it?'[16]

This is an imaginative attempt to suggest that our spiritual practice is not undertaken to attain a far-off goal, but rather to realize – to make real – the awakening we already possess. But it's not as simple as it sounds. Dogen continues with the warning that 'the way is as distant as heaven from earth, if the mind is lost in the confusion of likes and dislikes'. However much we may have understood, whatever wisdom or mental clarity we have gained, 'if your mind is still wandering, you have almost lost the way to awakening'. So we still need to practice like the Buddha and his followers down the ages, but in a way quite different from our conventional and logical approach: 'stop chasing words and studying phrases. Learn to step back and reflect instead upon yourself. Body and mind will fall away and your original face will appear.'[17]

Ritual, Monastics and Zen Masters

This deeply enigmatic text only begins to make sense when we gain some experience of meditation. So let's leave Dogen aside, at least for the moment. Which features of traditional Zen are central to a contemporary practice, and which might get in the way, especially for those who also identify themselves as Christians or secular humanists?

Perhaps the most obvious question here is about ritual. The monastic Zen tradition has many detailed practices, from the etiquette of how to enter, walk, bow and sit in the meditation hall, to the prostrations, chanting, candles, incense, bells and drums used in services. Fischer finds this helps cultivate 'gratitude, devotion, humility, concern for others', and chanting in Japanese honours the Zen tradition and its teachers. But he recognizes that many people dislike such services and rituals, and so may choose to practice Zen without them – as he sometimes does himself.[18]

Much of this ritual relates to the monastic community, and can seem irrelevant to everyday life. Monks visiting our Zen group tried to teach us to bow and make offerings and ring the bells correctly, and were disappointed by our lack of interest. As for chanting, many Buddhists chant in their own language, and we have seen that the Buddha asked his monks to express the dharma in the contemporary vernacular wherever they went.

Unofficial Buddhists may wish to discard most or all monastic ritual in any Zen-based practice, while not abandoning ritual on principle, as committed secular Buddhists might expect. We may still bow to an image of the Buddha, for example – not as a semi-divine being, but in recognition of the wisdom and compassion the statue represents, which is also the deepest part of our ourselves. We may also recite some short verses before meditation, to remind ourselves of what our practice is all about.

Without an elaborate monastic ritual, unofficial Buddhists will not need monastics to lead them. It can also be misleading to speak of Buddhist *monks* and *nuns* living in *monasteries*, as these are Christian terms. Modern Western Buddhist centres are often in rural locations, copying the Christian practice of monastic isolation, while early Buddhist communities were always close to the towns where their support came from. In the West we distinguish between celibate *monastics* and ordained *priests*, clergy with parish responsibilities. But Japanese Zen often combines these two roles, and in most Western Zen organizations male and female Zen teachers may marry, and are called *priests* to distinguish them from celibate *monks* or *nuns*. This is also misleading, as their role is radically different from that of Christian priests, who administer the sacraments to their congregation.

Traditional Zen schools see lineage and dharma transmission as an essential link between the Buddha himself and our current dharma teachers, showing respect and gratitude. But the Zen lineage was only created in seventh-century China, mainly to legitimize the Ch'an school of Mahayana Buddhism. The notion of dharma transmission could be seen as a further attempt to boost monastic authority. On the other hand, without some form of continuity, the teachings might have changed beyond recognition. But surely you don't need to *copy* your forebears to show them respect and gratitude. I will always be grateful to my father and my grandfather, but that doesn't mean I should become a bank manager or a Methodist minister.

Zen has a strong tradition of teacher and pupil, Zen master and Zen practitioner. Many look to their teacher for support and guidance, but this depends on the nature of the relationship. There is real value in experienced practitioners (whether we call them teachers or not) supporting less experienced practitioners – but in a spirit of spiritual friendship. The master-pupil relationship can lead people to rely on a teacher, rather than themselves, as their authority and refuge. It can also lead to hero-worship, and very occasionally to teachers who abuse their position of power. Fischer argues that while teachers and communities are valuable means of spiritual support, Zen can also be practised with no teachers or temples. Zen is fairly new in the West, and people are still exploring how it works in the modern world: 'Zen has to be different to fit us, but we have to be different to fit Zen.'[19]

Karma and Rebirth

Karma and rebirth may be awkward teachings for Westerners, who often see them as either alien to Western culture or simply irrelevant. We can accept the idea of cause and effect, where wise actions lead to good results and foolish actions leads to bad results, but it is much more difficult to imagine our actions here and now influencing a series of future lives. The idea that the innocent may be suffering because of their actions in previous lives sounds unfair or even offensive to many of us – and in any case it involves a leap of faith we may find impossible. The Buddha disagreed with the claim that our current painful experiences are the direct result only of our past actions. He pointed out that our suffering may be due to health problems, or the weather, or our careless behaviour, or even an assault, as well as the process of karma.[20]

Although his contemporaries usually believed in rebirth, it's not clear if the Buddha agreed with them. This is one of those metaphysical questions he tended to ignore. Our lives may well have a more lasting significance than we are aware of, but a Zen approach to rebirth might be to copy the Buddha and deconstruct the belief or ignore it, not engaging with the question rather than worrying about it. As Fischer suggests, we neither know what rebirth is, nor what we mean by believing in it. We don't even know what it is we are talking about.[21]

Four Elements of Zen Practice

If unofficial Buddhists can do without elaborate ritual or priests, if our teachers are spiritual friends rather than Zen masters, and if we don't have to believe in karma and rebirth – what's left? Which elements of Zen might be retained, cultivated or adapted for our contemporary spiritual practice?

While the Rinzai Zen school emphasizes direct exchanges between master and pupil, with a strenuous focus on paradoxical questions or riddles known as koans, the Soto Zen school has become the predominant form of Zen in the West. Soto Zen emphasizes four essential elements of practice: exploring and following the Zen precepts; practising daily meditation; developing compassionate behaviour; and realizing – making real rather than merely understanding – our 'Buddha nature'. We'll be looking at these topics in detail in Part Two, but it may be helpful to outline them here.

The growth of Western Zen in the 1960s counterculture of 'drugs, sex and rock and roll' has sometimes led people to assume that Zen had no moral rules. Nothing could be further from the truth. Zen's Ten Great Precepts draw on those practised from the earliest days of Buddhism. They encourage us to avoid killing, stealing, adultery, lying and intoxication, and to develop instead loving-kindness, generosity, faithfulness, truthfulness and mindfulness. Some practitioners recite these precepts at regular intervals, often preceded by 'taking refuge' in the Buddha, the dharma and the sangha, and by the more general undertaking to avoid harmful actions, practise skilful actions, and awaken the compassionate heart.

Second, the daily practice of *zazen* – seated meditation – is central to Zen. Since Zen doesn't require belief in either a deity or a set of doctrines, and *zazen* meditation emphasizes focusing simply on the present moment, Zen may be practised by Christians or Jews or secular humanists as well as Buddhists, without compromising their beliefs and practices. Simply being aware of our body and breathing is an enjoyable experience we rarely notice, and it can have a profound effect on the way we see things. Suzuki Roshi compared zazen to 'turning the soil', adding light and air so that plants can breathe and flourish.

Traditional Zen practitioners may attend a *sesshin*, an intense Zen retreat lasting a week or more, sitting in meditation for several hours each day. This is often seen as the standard for serious practitioners. Retreatants are encouraged to persevere and overcome their aversion to the physical pain of prolonged sitting. Many find these events beneficial. But after struggling through a series of week-long retreats, as the years wear on, we may find even this relatively mild ascetic practice feels too much like a hair-shirt Buddhism.

Third, the practice of *developing compassion* springs naturally from exploring and following the precepts, and from daily meditation, making us more aware of our emotional connection with other people. Everyone has the same deep wish to be peaceful and happy as we do, and we can hopefully find ways to help them with an open heart, rather than focusing obsessively on our own problems.

Following the precepts, practising meditation and developing compassion are simple enough to understand, though often much less easy to practice. But the fourth element – *realizing Buddha nature* – is more difficult to understand. It's sometimes expressed in theistic terms, as if there were some divine being or divine essence lurking in the background – but that's exactly what the Buddha *didn't* teach. Perhaps this Buddha nature is what D.T. Suzuki means by our essential 'inner purity and goodness' or what Kapleau calls our 'original perfection'.[22] Following Dogen, Fischer emphasizes that we practice Zen not as a long journey towards enlightenment, but rather to realize – to make real – the spiritual awakening which is inherently ours.[23] If this is still confusing – welcome again to Zen!

As well as these four elements, studying Zen teachings is also important, partly to challenge our ideas and theories in the light of our experience of meditation. This is very different from the familiar academic study we value so highly in the West. Here we study to support *practice*, rather than to pass exams. However fascinated they were by world religions, my Open University students still studied to write assignments and pass an exam to gain their second-level credit. But a sailor studies the weather forecast and the tide timetables for the more obvious reason of staying alive. This is perhaps how we should approach Buddhist teachings – as if our lives depend upon it. Zen texts may be deliberately opaque, encouraging readers to use the experience gained in their practice to reach beyond the meaning of the words on the page. In the introduction to his influential *Opening the Hand of Thought*, the Japanese Zen master Kosho Uchiyama (1912-98) underlines this clearly: 'What I want for you, the reader, is that you understand with your own intellect that Zen concerns the true depth of life that is beyond the reach of that intellect.'[24] Even though we now have access to a wide range of modern translations from ancient Theravada and Tibetan texts, as well as those from the Zen tradition, we still need to read between the lines.

There are less tangible aspects of Zen monastic life which could be helpful to us. These might include living more simply, consuming only what we really need, using our time wisely, leaving space for reflection rather than being constantly busy, slowing down, and perhaps turning our daily routine of cooking and cleaning into a form of working meditation. All this can appear useless from the viewpoint of the pervasive consumer culture which surrounds us in the West, bombarding us with adverts from every screen. Spiritual practice won't bring us perfect good looks, more wealth or greater intelligence. If we practice to get somewhere else or to gain something, it probably won't work. But if we are content to engage with spiritual practice *without* any goals, as Fischer says, if we are 'merely doing it to do it, it refreshes: it changes your life'.[25]

And we don't have to practice alone. Unless you live in the middle of nowhere, you can probably find like-minded people in your local area for a meditation group, whether they are Buddhists or Christians or neither. Practising together helps us to understand both ourselves and others, and so to soften the way we see and relate to each other. Letting go of our feeling of being separate, even briefly, can bring a profound awareness of a shared experience, a strong human need which lies at the centre of the spiritual life.

* * *

So now we turn back to these four elements: exploring and following the Zen precepts, practising daily meditation, developing compassion, and realizing – making real – the wisdom of 'Buddha nature', our own spiritual awakening. This is only another way of describing the Buddha's teaching – the path of morality, meditation and wisdom, which we will explore in detail in Part Two.

Part Two

Walking the Path

Chapter 5

Taking the First Steps

In Part One we tried to find a middle way between Asian and Western culture, between religious and secular viewpoints, and between an authoritative hierarchy and a more democratic approach based on personal experience. But where does the eightfold path begin, and what does it mean to *cultivate* the eightfold path? Can we find a middle way between the habitual over-indulgence which our consumer society encourages, and a hair-shirt asceticism which tries to ignore the everyday situations we find ourselves in? That's exactly what the Buddha recommended, when he found that neither of these extremes led to awakening. And how do we adapt or reinterpret the traditional elements in the eightfold path to help us find our way in the modern world? These are the questions we'll be looking at in Part Two.

When we begin to read about the eightfold path, it looks at first like a list of things which might help us get rid of suffering. Put your faith in the Four Noble Truths, be kind and compassionate, don't tell lies or steal things or misuse sex, earn an honest living, be positive, pay attention, and do lots of meditation. Right understanding, right thought, right speech, right action, right livelihood, right effort, right mindfulness and right concentration.

This is challenging enough – but there's clearly more to understand here. For a start, those titles can be confusing. The Pali *samma* does indeed mean *right*, or perfect or complete, but none of these seem the most appropriate term in English. *Right* and its implied opposite *wrong* seem to echo the biblical *Thou shalt not* commandments. *Perfect* suggests an ideal out of reach for ordinary mortals. And what would *complete* speech or action or livelihood mean?

It may be more helpful to take *samma* as 'wise' or 'appropriate' to suggest a more thoughtful engagement with each situation we find ourselves in. Or we might think of it instead as the opposite of foolish or unhelpful. It may be good to use different words in different aspects of the path, though this could perhaps lead to confusion. Throughout his *Eight Mindful Steps to Happiness*, the Sri Lankan monk Henepola Gunaratana uses the word *skilful*, suggesting each step as a practice to be developed, rather than a state of rightness or perfection to be sought after or achieved – a dynamic action rather than a passive concept.[1] *Skilful thinking* sounds much better to me than *right thought*.

The Buddha's teaching is often described as a threefold path of morality, meditation and wisdom. Trevor Ling compared morality and meditation to 'two strands of a rope which intertwine and strengthen each other' in a partnership which gradually leads towards wisdom.[2] I found this a helpful analogy, but it may give the misleading impression that some steps come before others. Perhaps we might see morality, meditation and wisdom rather as three sides of a triangle, each linked to the other two. Similarly, the more detailed eightfold path is not a series of stages on a journey, or eight objectives to be reached in turn, but a path where all the elements need to be developed together. We might see this as a gradual movement away from our habitual patterns of speaking, acting and thinking, towards more flexible responses. Or we could picture the eightfold path as a series of questions. What are wise and compassionate ways of viewing ourselves and the world? What effect does this have on the ways in which we speak, act and think?

We might well ask ourselves where this path is leading. It has often been described as a path of *transformation*. Phrases such as 'becoming a Buddha' or being 'united with ultimate truth' are frequently used to explain the spiritual goal of Buddhism, the destination of the eightfold path. But there is no mention of 'ultimate truth' in the Buddha's discourses – he showed no interest in such metaphysical questions – and Dogen's Zen meditation guidance includes the blunt phrase, 'Do not aim to become a Buddha'. It may seem odd to set out on a path without knowing where it is going, but in a sense that is exactly what we need to do. All we need to start with is an initial confidence that there is a path worth exploring.

However, it's still fair to ask why *skilful understanding* and *skilful thinking* are usually listed first. Shouldn't they come at the end, if moral behaviour and meditation practice eventually *lead* to wisdom? It's perhaps a question of the degree of understanding. Without that initial confidence, nobody would set out in the first place. The steps on the paths are all linked to each other, and little progress can be made without a certain amount of understanding, effort and mindfulness. If moral behaviour and meditation practice do indeed lead to wisdom, then eventually the confidence which prompts us to set out on the path will grow into a direct personal experience. We can see how this happens in our everyday life, when we first find the courage to ride a bicycle or to dive into the swimming pool – or when we first fall in love. So let's look at each of the eight aspects in turn, while remembering that we have to engage with them all at once, rather than one after the other. For each element, we need to explore what we're being encouraged to let go of, what we're hoping to take up or develop – and the relationship between them. Letting go of our habitual reactions may turn out to be more important than searching for ideal patterns of behaviour.

Skilful Understanding

Skilful understanding, often called *right view* (*samma ditthi* in Pali), is traditionally explained as understanding – perhaps initially simply accepting or taking on trust – the principles of karma and rebirth and the Four Noble Truths. This is the first step on the eightfold path, and is seen as the basic Buddhist worldview, the analysis of the human situation, the problem of the unsatisfactoriness of our lives, without which there would be no reason to set out on the path. More broadly, we might describe *samma ditthi* as 'wise perspective', an ability to reflect on our own values, and our capacity to *change*, whatever our current situation may be. The Buddha describes 'wrong view' or lack of understanding as the belief that good and bad actions have no corresponding results, and that there are no virtuous or spiritually awakened beings. This is the misguided belief that we can do exactly as we wish, with no repercussions, and that the spiritual life has no value.

Gunaratana describes karma as a 'simple principle of cause and effect' at the heart of Buddhist morality.[3] Unskilful behaviour brings unhappy outcomes, and skilful behaviour brings happy outcomes, in both our present and future lives. The traditional view is that our actions now will determine the kind of rebirth we earn for ourselves, either heavenly or hellish. A more secular approach would set rebirth aside and deal with cause and effect here and now. If we harm others, steal from them, exploit them sexually, or speak and act maliciously towards them, they will probably wish us ill, and may well contact their lawyers or the police. Sometimes they will respond more directly. When I was still in short trousers, I once punched a boy in the face, and he immediately punched me back again, twice as hard. That's the simple principle of cause and effect – actions really do have consequences!

There's also an underlying psychological causality at work here. When we feed our own feelings of anger and hatred, we immediately experience the suffering of those feelings, and so we reinforce these negative habits of mind. Similarly, when we cultivate our feelings of loving-kindness and compassion, there is both an immediate happiness and a reinforcement of these positive mental habits. The opening verses of the *Dhammapada* neatly illustrate how the thoughts which lie behind our actions bring their inevitable results:

> If you speak or act with a harmful thought,
> suffering will follow you, as the cart follows the ox.
> If you speak or act with a pure thought,
> happiness will follow you like a constant shadow.[4]

As we have seen, the Buddha pointed out that our current situation may be caused by the weather or our state of health, as well as our past actions. Our state of mind may be affected by going for a walk in the sunshine, or going down with flu in the winter, rather than how we behaved yesterday. But the underlying principle remains. If we stuff ourselves with food and get drunk in the evening, the next morning's indigestion and hangover will be entirely of our own making. Yes, actions have consequences, though the connection between any action and its result may be more tenuous and more complicated than a simple understanding of karma would imply.

An initial understanding or confidence in the Four Noble Truths is different from accepting them completely without question. If we see them as *doctrines*, we're likely to be drawn into a fixed idea of what is and isn't *true*, rather than keeping an open mind, a flexible approach to each new situation. One interpretation of *ditthi* is any kind of theory or value system or world view, so that *samma ditthi* might include seeing a view as *simply a view*, rather than an eternal truth. So skilful understanding includes looking honestly at our perceptions and opinions, our values and our view of the world, being prepared to challenge them rather than defending them dogmatically. This is why Stephen Batchelor's interpretation of the teaching as four *tasks* rather than four *truths* is so helpful, emphasizing that the eightfold path is about how we *behave* rather than what we *believe*. Our initial understanding or confidence is gradually confirmed through the personal experience of our practice, rather than simply a deepening of faith.

*　*　*

The Buddha warns his audience in the *Sammaditthi Sutta* and elsewhere to avoid what he describes as ten 'unwholesome' actions, prompted by the familiar roots of greed, hate and delusion, which lead only to misery in one form or another.[5] He divides these into physical, verbal and mental conduct. The three physical actions to avoid are killing or harming living beings, stealing or taking what is not given, and 'misconduct concerning sense-pleasures' (usually interpreted as sexual misbehaviour). The four verbal actions to avoid are false, slanderous, harsh and useless speech. The three mental actions to avoid are the familiar greed or covetousness, hate or ill-will, and deluded or false views, which can easily lead us into foolish speech and action. If we hate other people, we're likely to speak ill of them, and may wish to harm or even kill them. If we're greedy and deluded, we may well exploit others by stealing their property or using them to gratify our sexual desires.

Each of these foolish actions has its opposite in ten wise, 'wholesome', skilful or virtuous actions, prompted by generosity, loving-kindness and insight, and which will lead to a happy outcome. The three wise physical actions are to protect living beings and so develop loving-kindness; to give freely and so develop generosity; and to be faithful and self-restrained and so develop contentment. The four wise verbal actions are to speak only the truth and so develop truthfulness; to speak with kindness and so promote harmony; to speak softly and so develop gentleness; and to speak sensibly at the right time and so develop helpfulness. The three wise mental actions are to think generously and so develop contentment and tranquillity; to generate thoughts of goodwill and so develop compassion; and to think clearly and so develop insight and wisdom.

These ten wise and foolish actions form the basis for Buddhist ethics – the moral precepts common to all traditions, originally expressed as the Five Precepts of the Theravada, and later developed as the Ten Great Precepts of Zen. Each of them will be discussed in detail in the chapters which follow. At first they look like a list of *dos* and *don'ts*, some of them wearily familiar, rather like an Indian version of the Ten Commandments. But the Buddha is neither a quasi-divine being nor a prophetic spokesman. He is more like a wise physician, diagnosing the suffering of the human condition and prescribing the appropriate treatment. We might imagine him as an explorer, someone who has examined the paths we can take and discovered where each one comes from and where each one leads. But as he points out in the *Dhammapada*: 'You yourselves must make the effort, Buddhas only point the way.'[6]

Underlying the Buddhist view of the human situation are three characteristics which are seen as universal. First, as we have seen, there is the reality of *suffering* or *unsatisfactoriness*, the physical and mental sense of things not being as we would wish. This is largely because of the second characteristic, the fact of *impermanence*. Everything changes. Our bodies and minds change moment by moment, and almost all our cells are renewed within eight to ten years, some of them much more often. We are quite literally not the same people we were a decade ago. Although we can't observe the mountains rising or falling, and the continents colliding or drifting apart – since these are measured in geological time rather than in hours or days – they're still always changing.

Third, because everything is impermanent, including our own bodies and minds, we can have *no fixed and lasting self*, nothing we can call an eternal soul. What we like to think of as a fixed self is actually a temporary collection of physical and mental processes, which is always changing from moment to moment. All major religions except Buddhism have some form of soul-theory, and it's comforting to believe that in some way we and our loved ones continue to exist after our death. But where does the evidence for such beliefs come from? It's written into the sacred scriptures and woven into centuries of tradition. But scripture and tradition are two potential sources of truth which the Buddha advised the Kalamas not to rely upon, at least not without careful consideration. Christians and Buddhists may just have to agree to differ here. Despite well-meaning claims that all religions are really the same, they are in fact sometimes spectacularly different from each other!

Skilful Thinking

Skilful thinking, often called *right intention* or *right resolve* (*samma sankappa* in Pali), the second step on the eightfold path, is the wish to do something about these ten unwholesome actions and to start looking for and cultivating the qualities which underlie skilful actions instead. The

Buddha describes 'wrong intention', or unskilful or foolish thinking, as the driving force behind 'sensual desire ... ill will ... and cruelty'.[7] So *samma sankappa* is the intention or resolve to be free from all these negative mental states.

Skilful thinking includes a progressive letting go of unhelpful mental habits – the wish to surround ourselves with only pleasant things and experiences, or the more general tendency to adopt a negative frame of mind. This letting go can help make our minds more peaceful, with space to develop positive thoughts such as loving-kindness and compassion. Offering loving-kindness to ourselves and then to others – beginning with those close to us and eventually including even the most unfriendly people – may not bring them the peace and happiness we wish for them, but it's a practice which will change our own minds. *Change your mind*, as the monk suggested at my first Zen retreat. When we're consciously wishing people well, our hearts are open and we feel their suffering as if it were our own. Can such a change of mind prompt us to go beyond wishing them well? What can we do to help them?

The twelfth-century Tibetan monk, scholar and teacher Je Gampopa (1079–1153) described the root of loving-kindness as remembering the kindness done to us in the past. The kindest person of all here is our own mother, who fed and clothed us as helpless infants, wiped our bottoms, and taught us how to feed and dress ourselves, how to walk and how to speak.[8] As an adult, I sometimes had a difficult relationship with my own mother, and this passage always touches my heart, reminding me of her many kindnesses towards me when I was a child. And even if your mother did none of these kind things – even if she died in childbirth – she still gave you the gift of this precious human life. Gampopa says all sentient beings have been our mother in previous lifetimes, but we don't have to believe this in order to view all living beings in *this* world with the same loving-kindness shown to us by our mother. Gampopa is echoing the Buddha's advice in the foundational text, the *Metta Sutta*, in its beautiful lines on loving-kindness:

> Even as a mother protects with her life
> Her child, her only child,
> So with a boundless heart
> Should one cherish all living beings,
> Radiating kindness over the entire world.[9]

The wise intention behind skilful thinking prompts us to examine our actions, to see if they are adding to or reducing the suffering experienced by others or by ourselves. This wise intention can also help us to distance ourselves from our negative thoughts and emotions. Whenever they arise – the fear and jealousy, the anger and ill-will – we tend to make things worse by blaming ourselves. *I shouldn't feel jealous or angry, I must be a bad person.* There is no need to beat ourselves up like this. We don't have to *identify* ourselves with these emotions. The Buddha reminds us that we cannot always control our feelings, but we can say: 'This is not mine; this is not what I really am; this is not my self.'[10]

Stephen Batchelor points out that *sankappa* comes from a verb meaning to think about or to imagine, and hence to create or build. This implies that our skilful thinking may include our imaginative and creative abilities, as well as the simple wish to avoid foolish actions and develop wise actions.[11] This underlines for me the idea of *cultivating* the path – making our own path ourselves by walking on it, rather than following a set of instructions (however authoritative) which applies to all wanderers. This involves imagining – or perhaps *reimagining* – each element of the eightfold path, as other Buddhist cultures have always done over the centuries, to support our practice in contemporary Western societies, where we find ourselves today.

We'll come back to skilful understanding and skilful thinking in Chapter 11. They begin as the initial confidence needed to set out on a spiritual journey – but we may eventually be able to see them as the wisdom gained by having walked along the path. Meanwhile, Martine Batchelor suggests three qualities which can help us.[12] We need *great faith* – but faith in our own potential, our ability to practice, rather than faith that someone else can do the work for us. We need *great courage* – to give us the energy to practise, the determination to keep on letting go of our habitual reactions. We also need *great questioning* – not to ask how well we are doing, but coming back again and again to examine how we should best proceed on the eightfold path. That's when we start asking ourselves about *skilful action*.

Chapter 6

Cultivating Compassionate Behaviour

The Buddha encourages us in the *Metta Sutta* to 'cherish all living beings, radiating kindness over the entire world'. But before these famous words on loving-kindness, he makes it clear that ethical behaviour is the basis for all our actions:

This is what should be done
By one who is skilled in goodness,
And who knows the path of peace.[1]

What does it mean to be *skilled in goodness*? How should I avoid harmful actions and develop skilful actions? To answer these questions, Buddhists have always relied on the Five Precepts, the moral principles common to all traditions. They relate closely to the wise and unwise actions the Buddha explained, and will be explored in the next two chapters. The next aspect of the eightfold path, skilful or wise action (*samma kammanta* in Pali), is at the heart of our individual behaviour, our relationships, and the way we live in communities.

We tend to think of ethical behaviour either as commandments to be obeyed or as promises to keep; but the Buddhist precepts are deliberately phrased instead as *training rules*, recognizing that it takes time and effort to become skilled in goodness. If precepts are instructions or promises made, our responses will tend to rely on either obedience or will power. We may then feel proud of our ability to *keep* the precepts, or ashamed if we *break* them – but neither of these emotional reactions are very helpful. Instead we can see the precepts more as *guidelines*, paths which can lead us away from foolish and harmful actions, and towards more wise and skilful behaviour.

Each of the Five Precepts, each area of our behaviour, prompts us to ask ourselves questions. What is it we need to let go of, to avoid? What is the skilful behaviour we need to take up instead? And how do we *engage* with this precept, considering both the intentions behind our actions and the results which follow? We need to see *why* we behave foolishly, using the precepts to discover more about ourselves. As well as warning us when we are heading towards harmful actions, they can help us see how our habitual reactions arise, and how we can begin to let go of them. That's when the precepts can go beyond our intellectual understanding of wise and foolish actions, beginning to enter our hearts, to become truly part of our innermost being.

We have to be prepared for surprises. The precepts may lead us into places we're not prepared for, places we don't want to visit, hidden areas of our behaviour or our prejudices, the habits we're comfortable with and really don't want to change. The process of looking closely at our actions, our speech and our thoughts, helps us to see our habitual reactions, and so to let go of them and respond more creatively to whatever situation we are in.

This is not just about my personal behaviour. As we have seen, the Buddha sets out in the *Sigalaka Sutta* the responsibilities of children and parents, pupils and teachers, husbands and wives, employers and employees, and householders and monastics.[2] This social context includes you and me as family members, as friends and neighbours, and as community groups from church congregations to yoga classes, from mothers and toddlers to lunch clubs for senior citizens. The work context includes you and me as colleagues, as workers and bosses, as tradespeople and shop assistants, as clients and customers, from the window cleaner to the multinational company. The broader political and environmental context also includes you and me as constituents and campaigners. How do we relate to our local and national representatives, to our government's policies, and to international questions, including how all of us look after the planet?

So let's consider each of these ten precepts in turn, but not just as a list of harmful actions to avoid. They can also be warning signals to remind us, and also what the American Zen teacher Diane Eshin Rizzetto calls 'keys to self-discovery', helping us to examine both our actions and the thoughts which lie behind them, so that they can help us to unlock 'our deepest capacity for love, empathy, fairness and joy'.[3]

Cultivating Loving-Kindness

The first precept, seen in all Buddhist traditions as the most important, is the firm intention not to kill or harm any humans or animals, but instead to help and protect them. The earliest version, still used in the Theravada tradition, is: *I undertake the rule of training to refrain from harming living beings.* Western Zen groups sometimes phrase this precept either as a command – *Refrain from destroying life* – or as a vow or promise – *I will refrain from killing* – or again as a positive aspiration – *I take up the way of supporting life.*

What's the difference between *not killing* and *not harming* living beings? We may not imagine ourselves killing anyone, but most of us have sometimes caused other people harm with our thoughtless and selfish behaviour. And it's not just humans. *Living beings* includes mammals, birds and fish and even insects. We may open the window to let a wasp out, and we probably never attack any mammals, birds or fish. But if we choose to eat their flesh, someone has to kill them on our behalf. Does that count?

I thought at first that being a pacifist vegetarian would do the trick. This reminded me of arguments with my father, who fought in the Second World War, and told me if *his* generation had been pacifists, we would all be ruled by the Nazis. This had no effect on an omniscient fifteen-year-old who knew that killing was *obviously always wrong*. Now I realise it may not be so simple. In extreme situations – preventing genocide or crimes against humanity – taking someone's life may possibly be the least-worst option. Isn't that exactly what my father was doing, trying to bring an end to the holocaust, as well as protecting Britain from invasion?

Buddhist tradition teaches that soldiers who die in battle will be reborn in hell or as animals. We don't have to believe in karma or rebirth to see soldiers coming back from war zones with terrible post-traumatic stress, because of what they have seen and done. Some may indeed find their experience after the conflict is not unlike being reborn in hell.

Vegetarianism looks like a much simpler choice. Don't kill animals to eat them, since we wish not to harm them, we don't *need* meat or fish, and a veggie diet may be heathier for us and much better for the environment. What about dairy products? If we drink milk or eat cheese, we're probably complicit in the killing of countless unwanted male calves. And eating eggs deprives chickens of life. Of course if everyone suddenly went vegan, there would be millions of cattle, sheep and pigs surplus to requirements. But it's not going to happen any day soon.

Are we making these ethical choices to protect living beings? Perhaps our motivation is more selfish, giving up meat and fish to feel better about ourselves, to think of ourselves as being pure and righteous. This precept can certainly point us in the direction of not harming other humans and animals, but we need to be clear about *why* we wish to protect them. There's an enlightened self-interest here. As the Buddha says in the *Dhammapada*: 'If we harm living beings who – like us – long for happiness, we will never find happiness ourselves.'[4]

This first precept covers many areas, from the smallest life forms – the germs we have to kill to protect our own health – to a wide range of ethical questions. At the beginning of life, we may have to consider abortion and the use of stem cells. At the end of life, we may wonder if euthanasia is permissible, after doing all we can for the terminally ill. There are questions about how we conduct our wars, how we punish our criminals, and how we pollute our planet and so threaten the lives of all who live here. These are complex issues. We may believe firmly that all life is sacred – from conception to the last breath – but our confidence can sometimes be challenged by events. How should we act compassionately when we have created the unwanted pregnancy ourselves – or when our daughter or our sister is considering an abortion? How should we respond when the person in constant pain is our own mother or father – or if we ourselves long for death as a release from suffering?

We can harm people in many ways, from physical violence to cheating or deceiving them, or belittling their beliefs and ideas. But Buddhist teaching sees all of these as *mistakes* rather than transgressions – there's no concept of sin or divine commandments or judgement. We're simply responsible for our own actions, which will have consequences either now or later. We have to make judgements all the time, working out in each situation which is the wisest action to take – or to avoid taking – in our behaviour towards other living beings.

As soon as we have the wish to avoid harming, we open the way towards compassionate behaviour, the wish to help and protect others. The eighth-century Buddhist scholar and poet Shantideva encourages us to regard all our fellow creatures as the same as ourselves, with the same sorrows and joys as we have. He suggests that we should love and care for all our fellow living beings as if they were our own hands and feet, vital parts of our own body, rather than being separated from us.[5]

Again there is an enlightened self-interest. If we support and care for those who – like us – long for happiness, we will inevitably find it for ourselves.

This is not just about a personal change of heart. Several countries – including our own – have enough nuclear weapons to kill millions of people, but still fail to protect their citizens and their children from poverty. Our whole ecosystem is under threat from the climate change caused by widespread pollution and deforestation. We may wish to campaign with others for a change of heart from our governments and corporations. What level of protest or civil disobedience can we justify? Neither ending slavery nor achieving votes for women were achieved just by asking nicely. If we could disable a nuclear warhead, should we be charged with terrorism or given a peace prize?

The Buddha offers clear advice in the *Metta Sutta*: 'Let none through anger or ill-will wish harm upon another'.[6] We are all aware of this anger and ill-will, which bubbles up inside us from time to time, where one way or another we wish someone else harm. These are the familiar poisons of greed, hate and delusion. Can we learn to let go of them, and begin to develop their opposites – generosity, loving-kindness and compassion? As we have seen, Gampopa suggests developing loving-kindness by viewing all beings as your own mother, and he says compassion may be similarly cultivated. If you saw your mother cold and hungry, or weakened by age and sickness, you would naturally feel compassion for her. Since other beings are currently suffering like this, we should cultivate the same compassion towards them, wishing them all to be free from suffering and its causes.[7] When loving-kindness and compassion are fully developed, we no longer cherish ourselves more than others, as we no longer see them as separate from us. This is when we become skilled in goodness.

Thinking of our actions and the mental states which lie behind them, perhaps we can combine the negative and positive aspects of the first precept:

Letting go of the wish to harm others, I take up the way of loving-kindness, supporting and protecting living beings.

Cultivating Generosity

The second precept is the wish to avoid selfish behaviour and to develop generosity instead. The original version is: *I undertake the rule of training to refrain from taking what is not given.* This is usually understood simply as not stealing. Again, Western Zen groups may express this as a command – *Do not steal* – or as a promise or vow – *I will refrain from stealing.* We're only prompted to steal from others when we imagine we're incomplete and we need to grasp for more. The version used at the Bay Center in Oakland, California, neatly combines the original and the positive response: *I take up the way of taking only what is freely given and giving freely of all that I can.*[8] This hints at the idea of developing respect for others and their property, and exchanging greediness and grasping for contentment and generosity – letting go of our habitual attachment to things.

It sounds simple at least to avoid stealing. Surely we're all honest – we're not muggers or bank robbers! If we pick up someone's lost purse or wallet, do we hand it in? Of course we do. But what about our tax returns? Maximizing our expenses to pay less will reduce funding for schools and hospitals. Again this comes down to our own responsibility for our actions, particularly at work, and we'll come back to this in Chapter 8. We can avoid theft or fraud relatively easily, but perhaps we're making illicit copies of documents or films or software – that's taking what's not given, isn't it? Those lengthy coffee breaks are taking your employer's time, and continual grumbling might be taking away your listener's peace of mind – which they would surely not wish to give you.

We're often taking what's not given from our environment. If we drive a petrol or diesel car, own a mobile phone, and use electricity generated by fossil fuels, we're taking oil and mineral resources from a planet which cannot renew them, and polluting the air we all breathe. We're cutting down forests much faster than we're replanting them, often to clear land for cattle, which we then slaughter and eat. Rich nations (that means us) often behave as if they *own* these resources, while poorer nations tend to suffer the worst consequences of rising temperatures and rising sea levels. We can use this precept to avoid dishonesty, to respect others and their needs, becoming less self-centred and developing generosity. But are we generous enough to run our central heating and air-conditioning from renewable resources? Are we generous enough to give up our cars and our mobile phones?

More generally, can we imagine ourselves *using less stuff*? However precious our possessions are, acquiring more of them is not going to ensure our happiness. Looking after them rather than discarding and replacing them – and so using Earth's finite resources more sparingly – might bring us a greater sense of satisfaction, remembering that these resources have to be shared with everyone else.

If we see ourselves as separate from others, there will always be that obsessive tendency to grasp whatever we can for ourselves, and to cling onto our possessions, suspicious that others will want to take them from us. The electronic gates to a large house or a wealthy community separate those inside from the surrounding area, both literally and symbolically. If we can start to see this idea of separateness as a *delusion*, these grasping habits may start to fall away. We're all dependent on each other for everything – from the basic needs of our food and clothing and shelter to our heart-felt wishes to love and to be loved. This is where the positive aspect of engaging with the second precept takes over, and our meanness and grasping can hopefully start to give way to generosity.

We may be held back by our habitual ideas of needing things, or being entitled to have the things we want. We imagine that if we don't get them, we're somehow failures or powerless, and that can make us feel vulnerable. Diane Rizzetto calls this 'the belief of *not-enough-ness* … the assumption that there is something to attain', which sits at the heart of working with this precept.[9] We're often judged by our *achievements* – our qualifications, work status, homes and possessions – and we can judge ourselves by these standards too. Who hasn't felt pleased with themselves after passing an exam, gaining a promotion, or buying a new car? I was delighted to complete my PhD, but I was still the same old mixture of foolish and wise actions, kind and unkind thoughts – and certainly no more intelligent. We can even tell ourselves that we should be gaining something from our spiritual practice: *I've been meditating for years, so shouldn't I be much closer to nirvana?* This is the same delusional idea of lacking something.

The idea of *giving freely* opens up searching questions. How ready are we to offer our time and energy to others, or our skills and expertise? Do we limit how much we offer, measuring out our generosity and expecting repayment in kind – or at least *gratitude* from the other person? That's not giving freely, that's *making a deal*, where we're somehow out of pocket if there's no return for our generosity. And there's another side to this deal. If someone offers us their time and energy, or their advice – or even their friendship – we may feel uncomfortable in accepting this as a gift. Surely we ought to repay their kindness, to offer them something in return, or they will think we are ungrateful? None of this is giving freely, showing the compassion both to give and to receive with an open heart.

The Buddha describes 'accomplishment in generosity' as having 'a mind free from the stain of miserliness, freely generous, open-handed ... delighting in giving and sharing'.[10] This begins with not stealing, but extends into a gradual weakening of our habitual possessiveness, so that we can *enjoy* sharing our resources with others, eventually developing that pervasive generosity which doesn't see the other person as different from myself.

Thinking of our wish to change both our behaviour and the underlying thoughts and emotions which affect how we relate to other people, perhaps we can combine the negative and positive aspects of the second precept:

> *Letting go of selfish greed, I take up the way of generosity,*
> *the way of giving freely all that I can.*

Cultivating Contentment

The third precept is usually translated as avoiding sexual misconduct, interpreted as being faithful in relationships, and avoiding any sexual exploitation or abuse. This helps us again in developing respect for others, and not indulging in activities which would harm them. The precept is expressed in contemporary Zen organizations as *I will refrain from abusing sexuality*, or more positively as *I take up the way of not misusing sex*.

There are different interpretations of sexual misconduct. The Pali texts explain that men should not have sex with women who are married, betrothed, under-age or close relatives – and women should only have sex with their husbands. It's no surprise to find one rule for the boys and another for the girls in a patriarchal society like ancient India. But the underlying bias is alive and well in the modern world, as women are only too well aware, where the terms *single mothers* and *single fathers* tend to prompt quite different reactions.

It's difficult to ignore a modern media industry which uses sexual imagery to sell motor cars as well as beauty products, bombarding us with pictures of attractive and alluring young women and men. Sex sells things, because our sexual energy is powerful, and difficult to resist or to ignore. We need to acknowledge and understand our sexual feelings, to look at them clearly, so that we are able to avoid any activity which exploits people, putting our own selfish pleasure before the feelings of others. We are sometimes tempted to use sexual relationships to distract us from our loneliness, to satisfy our longing to be loved – or to make us feel desirable, with the power to attract sexual partners. But this is all an illusion based on our own ego-needs. The misuse of intimate relationships damages both the people directly involved and those around them, spreading feelings of betrayal and manipulation.

This precept encourages us not only to avoid harming other people, but to use our sexual energy wisely in whatever situation we may be in. For many of us, this means a loving relationship with a partner, based on faithfulness and trust, where a deep intimacy can develop, bringing both partners great happiness. For others, it may mean a celibate lifestyle, still acknowledging sexual feelings but choosing not to act on them. These are not the only choices of lifestyle of course, and monogamy or celibacy may themselves be undertaken as temporary rather than permanent arrangements. Whatever we choose, this means having an open heart, being aware of other people and their feelings. As the American Zen teacher Reb Anderson (b. 1943) explains, grasping our sexual passion burns us up and harms others, while denial freezes us and harms others. 'But if we just stay close to it ... neither identifying with nor distancing ourselves from our sexuality, then we gradually become intimate with it'.[11] With that balanced approach, we may be able to bring a more loving care into our relationships, whether they are temporary or lifelong.

Almost all the literature limits this precept to sexual behaviour. But the original Pali version is much broader: *I undertake the rule of training to refrain from misconduct concerning sense-pleasures.* This sounds like a euphemism for adultery, promiscuity or sexual abuse, but it has far wider implications for our daily life. Sensuality is not all about sex. We have five senses – six if you include the activity of the mind – and we can easily misuse any or all of them.

We think of sight and hearing as our most obvious senses, the ones we value most highly and are most afraid of losing. As well as watching pornography, watching anything to excess is foolish. There's a big difference between giving an interesting TV programme or film our full attention, and watching merely to pass the time, or to divert ourselves from our daily problems. If we're slumped in front of the screen all evening, ploughing our way through box-sets of popular dramas, this can easily become addictive behaviour which is difficult to change. Similarly with hearing, if we have music in our ears all the time – whether it's Taylor Swift or the Arctic Monkeys, The Beatles or Beethoven – we're distracted from what's going on around us, blotting out the real world with our favourite sounds. This can even become an obsessional search for quality, looking for the perfect cinematic experience or the most exquisite sound reproduction.

Our senses of smell and taste can also be used in wise or foolish ways. We're easily repelled by unpleasant odours, we enjoy the enticing smells coming from the kitchen, and we like to smell nice ourselves. But smell and taste can overwhelm us, leading us to overeat, to stuff ourselves with food, feeling that we always need more. Those occasional glasses of wine or beer can easily become habit-forming, and if we're drinking to forget our problems, we may create new ones with our drunken behaviour. Again we may confuse quality with quantity. When we've found a restaurant serving the perfect meal with the best wine, we may want this experience more often, perhaps with extra helpings and another bottle.

Watching our sense of touch can also be interesting. We all want our clothes and bedding to be comfortable, and there is tactile fun to be had in driving a car or riding a bicycle. But again it's easy to be drawn into more obsessional behaviour, where we yearn for fine woollen garments or silk sheets, and a newer machine which will go even faster.

Then there's the mind and its thoughts. It's so easy to *indulge* the weird narratives the mind throws up, playing the tape and following the story, rather than asking ourselves whether the thoughts are actually true. When a friend says something we find annoying, we may be tempted to speak sharply in return. Do we shout at him and indulge our irritation, or keep silent and blame ourselves for having the unworthy thought in the first place? No, these are only thoughts – they are just what the mind throws up, they don't mean we're bad people. As a teenager, our priest warned us against 'impure thoughts' – as if we could *force* ourselves not to think about sex when we were fifteen! But we can choose not to trust our thoughts, and more importantly not to act on them.

We can easily waste our mental energy on trivial things. Are we really doing crosswords and Sudoku to stave off Alzheimer's, or just to while away the next half hour? Dogen's words are a stern warning we may not wish to hear: 'You have received a precious human life: do not waste your time. What use are fleeting pleasures? Our life is like a flash of lightning, transient and illusory – suddenly it is gone.'[12]

Back in front of the TV with a few beers and a bag of tasty snacks, we may be indulging and misusing all our senses at once. There's the sight and sound of the rubbish on the screen, the taste and touch and smell of the goodies we're gobbling, and the mental delusions that we need to keep our calorie intake up, and that the film will bring us lasting happiness. If we're glued to our mobile phones, scrolling through social media, posting and receiving messages and surfing the internet, we're probably misusing our eyes and ears and minds all over again.

And *why* are we doing all this? It's the self-centred *neediness* of obsessional behaviour, coupled with the wish to blot out or ignore the real world, which can appear unpleasant or painful or just boring. Much of this activity is simply propping up our ego, so that we can continue to believe that we're always happy and popular and well-informed.

As well as suggesting a range of actions to avoid, this precept can steer us towards more positive behaviour. Instead of indulging in sense-pleasures – whatever they may be – we're encouraged to develop a wise contentment and restraint. The Buddha underlines this again in the *Metta Sutta*, reminding us that to be 'skilled in goodness' we also need to be 'contented and easily satisfied'.[13] This has wider implications than developing faithfulness in sexual relationships. Underlying all our sensual desires is that sense of *grasping* which can easily become obsessional or even addictive. Filling ourselves up with food, filling our ears with music, and filling our eyes and brains with information are all examples of greediness – but they're also distractions from looking at what is going on. We're always grabbing at things, trying to get hold of stuff from *out there*, to make us feel better *in here*.

Of course this doesn't mean we have to live on bread and water. We can still enjoy food and drink, TV programmes and our favourite music, as well as art galleries and beautiful landscapes and holidays. We don't have to lead a celibate or ascetic life, since we're not monastics. Instead we should be aware of how we're using our senses, so that we're not drawn into forms of compulsive behaviour – including compulsive thinking. It's all too easy to indulge our prejudices about the government and multinational corporations. We may need to cut down on the righteous indignation, as well as the alcohol and the junk food.

As before, we can perhaps combine the negative and positive aspects of the third precept:

Letting go of selfish sensuality, I take up the way of contentment, self-restraint and faithfulness, treating all beings with respect and dignity.

Cultivating a Clear Mind

The fifth precept is the one most often forgotten or quietly ignored. (We'll consider the fourth precept about lying and truthfulness in the next chapter.) Translated literally, the Pali version sounds quaint and pedantic: *I undertake the rule of training to refrain from liquors which engender slothfulness.* Yes, this is about the demon drink. As before, it's a freely undertaken training rule, rather than signing a pledge, and many Buddhists are not teetotallers. It's fine to agree to refrain from killing, stealing, adultery and lying – but if I can't even have a beer or a glass of wine, maybe Buddhism's eightfold path is not for me after all?

On the other hand, it's not so easy to remain kind and generous, let alone faithful and truthful, when we're drunk. Most of us have been there, haven't we? Can you remember some of the things you said or did when under the influence, either years ago as immature teenagers, or more recently as supposedly responsible adults? Embarrassing or what?

The precept is often expressed more widely as refraining from *drink or drugs which cloud the mind*. Most Zen groups express this as avoiding taking or selling alcohol or recreational drugs. The mind can become clouded easily enough without intoxicants, and some groups extend this precept to refer to indulging in delusive thinking, and encouraging others to do so. This may be expressed as not *selling the wine of delusion*, or more prosaically and more positively as *I take up the way of cultivating a clear mind*.

Why do we take intoxicants in the first place? When we feel miserable, drinking alcohol takes that feeling away for a while. If we want to feel calmer or more excited, various psychoactive substances – legal or illegal – will temporarily do the trick. But these only deal with the *symptoms* of our unhappiness or anxiety, not the *causes*. When we sober up or come down from the drug-induced high, the problem's still there. We may become addicted to drink or drugs, always topping them up to keep the demons at bay. But the only way to solve our problems – to escape from the suffering – is to look at the problems with a clear mind.

This is often about *dependence*. If we can't do without regular doses of alcohol or drugs, we're not independent. If we allow ourselves to become intoxicated with delusive thinking – such as conspiracy theories or paranoia – our minds are not free. We might even become intoxicated with spiritual teachings, convinced that we've found the ultimate truth, and exhilarated by our wonderful discoveries. In the parable of the raft, the Buddha explains that even his teaching is only for crossing the river, not for carrying away on your back into the jungle.[14] He refers instead to people becoming independent in the dharma, responsible for their own spiritual practice, rather than following blindly – however inspiring the teaching may be.

We need to be honest with ourselves about the possible results of indulging in drink or drugs or delusive thinking, which may lead to addictive or dependent behaviour. Without getting too precious about the idea that my body is a temple, we can reflect on how these intoxicants can affect our well-being, from permanent liver damage to scrambling our brains.

This precept originally centred on the use of alcohol, but we now take it to include all forms of recreational drugs, from occasional marijuana to heroin addiction. But there are many other ways of clouding the mind. We can use almost any substance or any activity to take our minds away from the present moment, the place where we are now, which often seems to be lacking something that we feel we need. But of course here – in the present moment – is the only real place and time we have.

One of my diversionary tactics is watching TV in the evening. Why look at stuff I've seen before? I could be doing something useful or more creative, reading or listening to music or tidying up. What if I did something else this evening? How would I experience not watching TV? Another habit is nibbling. I convince myself that I still feel hungry after our evening meal, so later on I'll have some cheese and biscuits. Do I need extra sustenance? No, it's sheer delusive greed. And I want to lose weight, don't I? Let's not get obsessional about that either. All of these habits are about *neediness* – needing to divert my attention, needing to fill myself up, needing to look slimmer. Can I let go of each of them?

We use the analogy of *clouding the mind* with good cause. The Tibetan Buddhist tradition teaches that the mind is naturally clear and pure, like bright blue sky directly above us on a sunny day. But as the weather changes, the clouds obscure this wonderful blue sky and we may be tempted to forget about it. In the same way we can get used to the mind being confused, almost as if that is our normal state. But of course the clear mind is still there, still available to us, like the clear sky behind the clouds – if we are prepared to look for it.

Some people claim to have deep spiritual experiences when taking recreational drugs. (Maybe it was smoking marijuana many years ago which first made me aware of different states of mind, and led me to try meditation.) And some ancient traditions have used various psychedelic substances as tools for spiritual development. But apart from the terrible harm drugs can do – and the persistent danger of being arrested – all the weird and wonderful experiences they bring are only temporary. Drugs don't help us to escape from suffering, or to change our habitual greed, hate and delusion into generosity, loving-kindness and insight.

The medicinal use of drugs to restore the equilibrium of the body or the mind is another matter. Many years ago I was suffering from depression, and mentioned this clouding-the-mind precept as my friendly doctor was about to prescribe antidepressants. He skilfully suggested that these pills would instead help to *uncloud* the mind. Since I lacked the capacity to restore my mental equilibrium unaided, I should take them until I was able to look more clearly at the *causes* of the depressive episode. And this is what happened. There was an old store of unrecognized grief which had to be acknowledged and worked through. This reminded me that the wise can appear anywhere – whether we call them bodhisattvas or guardian angels – and whether they are wearing a Buddhist or Christian or medical label.

Of course the main reason for avoiding intoxicants is that we are trying to let go of our delusions and to develop *mindfulness* – of which more later in Chapter 9. Mindfulness can help us identify the tricks we use in order to avoid any continuous awareness of reality – either by dulling our senses with drink, or by slumping in front of the TV each evening. Again I remember the gaze of that kindly monk on my first Zen retreat: *Change your mind!*

As before, the negative and positive aspects of this fifth precept can be combined, reflecting our actions and the thoughts behind them:

> *Letting go of intoxicants and delusive thinking, I take up the way of mindfulness, the way of cultivating a clear mind.*

* * *

If we can learn to avoid harming living beings and develop loving-kindness, to avoid stealing from them and develop generosity, to avoid misusing all our senses and develop contentment and faithfulness, and to avoid clouding the mind with drink and drugs, developing a clear mind instead – all this is skilful or wise action. Actions often really do speak louder than words, which is why I've reversed the usual order of the eightfold path here. But now it's time to look at skilful speech.

Chapter 7

The Power of Speech

Our ability to make sounds which have meaning, expressing the simplest and the most complex ideas, allows us to communicate with each other, and this forms the basis of human culture. All the more reason to speak wisely rather than foolishly. As we have seen, the Buddha encouraged people to avoid false, slanderous, harsh and useless speech, and to practise truthful, kindly, gentle and helpful speech instead.[1] We were all brought up not to tell lies, but we still sometimes say the wrong thing at the wrong time. How can we avoid misleading or hurting people with the words we use? What would it mean to develop *skilful speech*?

Developing Truthfulness

The most obvious aspect of wise speech is avoiding lies and telling the truth. The fourth precept – the one we missed out in the last chapter – is often seen as second only to the first precept of not harming living beings. With practice, we can develop the habit of showing loving-kindness towards them in our speech as well as our actions. This precept, like the others, may be phrased as an imperative – *Do not say that which is untrue* – or as a promise or vow – *I will refrain from speaking untruthfully*. The original is *I undertake the rule of training to refrain from speaking falsely*, and this is picked up in modern Zen versions – *I take up the way of speaking truthfully* – or more imaginatively – *Listening and speaking from the heart*.

When we tell lies, we're often trying to protect our own image. The naughty child tries to shift the blame onto another, partly to escape punishment, but also to preserve their reputation and their own view of themselves. As adults, we still want to think well of ourselves as kindly and helpful people, so we play down or deny the mean or unfriendly things we say. *No, I didn't start the argument – you did!* This precept can help us to look closely at the ways in which we avoid telling the truth, and the self-centred reasons behind our attempts to deceive others. Lying undermines our relationships with other people, as they won't know who to trust. And we often speak without really knowing what we're talking about, either to persuade people that we know more than we do, or just to avoid those awkward silences. We could make a start here by really listening to ourselves, being more aware of what we are saying, and how the tone of our voice will appear to others.

Speaking falsely is broader than deliberate lying and deception. It's quite possible to make a statement which is completely true and still dishonest. Governments sometimes claim to be spending *more* on healthcare and education, while an ageing population and an increased birth rate means they are spending *less* for each patient and each student. That's deliberately deceptive. So false speech includes both lying and any exaggeration or misleading comment. And the more we deceive others, the less we can see the truth clearly for ourselves. We still tell ourselves we are honest, which only increases our deluded view of ourselves. We can also speak falsely by remaining silent, if we fail to warn someone who is stepping into danger – literally or metaphorically – or even if we don't own up about eating all the biscuits.

Truthful speech is an essential requirement for any spiritual life, fostering deeper qualities of truthfulness and honesty. If we always speak honestly and truthfully, it becomes habitual, and those to whom we speak know they can trust us. The Buddha reminds his followers repeatedly that someone who avoids all forms of false speech will be known as 'a truth-speaker, one to be relied on, trustworthy, dependable, not a deceiver of the world'.[2] Remembering how easily we can be hurt, or our reputation damaged, by someone speaking falsely about us, we will naturally refrain from speaking falsely about them. And we will not only tell the truth ourselves, but encourage others to do so.

Of course developing truthfulness is more than a personal responsibility. It's vitally important in the social context of our family, our friends and neighbours, and our local community – and at work with our colleagues and managers, our clients and customers, and the wider organizations we have dealings with. In public life, truthful speech is an essential part of a stable society. Without it, even the rule of law is undermined, if witnesses cannot be trusted in court. Truthfulness can help establish – or perhaps re-establish – trust in politicians and governments, and trust between nations.

Again we can try to combine the positive and negative aspects of the fourth precept:

> *Letting go of deceitful speech, I take up the way of truthfulness, listening and speaking from the heart.*

Developing Kindly, Gentle and Helpful Speech

Skilful speech is much wider than avoiding lying and developing truthfulness, and the Buddha gives three further examples of foolish speech to avoid. The first of these is malicious speech, which disturbs harmonious relationships between people. The phrase 'with malice aforethought' is used to indicate the premeditated wish to kill or injure someone, but it also illustrates the wish to harm someone by what we say. Malicious speech comes from a feeling of ill-will towards someone, and often involves lying about them, even slandering them, and perhaps prompting them to call their lawyers. At the very least, such speech causes a lack of trust, and may have a powerful effect on both individuals and communities. It divides people from each other, robbing them of their good name and causing discord. If we speak with malice, it will inevitably rebound on us, when people discover we were insulting or slandering them. Whose good name will suffer then?

Think how unpleasant it would be if someone drove a wedge between us and our friends by slandering one of us. If we keep this in mind, we will naturally avoid doing the same to them, and pull ourselves up short when we're tempted to speak ill of anyone. Of course we can still criticize someone where this is justified, though we need to be careful about both our intention and how we express ourselves here.

Kindly speech – speaking from a mind of kindness rather than malice – is a difficult habit to develop and maintain, but it has a powerful effect, promoting harmony. The Buddha gives the example of someone who hears something in confidence, but does not maliciously repeat it elsewhere, knowing that it would only sow division. Anyone who is able instead to develop kindly speech, free of all malice, will become 'one who reunites those who are divided, a promoter of friendships, who enjoys concord ... a speaker of words that promote concord'.[3]

* * *

Harsh or rude speech, shouting and swearing at people, only brings anger and discord in return, and can easily lead to physical violence. Speaking aggressively only hurts and offends people, belittling them with sarcasm or obscenities. When we shout at people we are propping up our own ego again, telling ourselves that we're right and they're wrong. It's also an assertion of power or authority. If we believe we're justified in shouting at someone, there's a righteous indignation behind our harsh words. We expect them to apologize. If they're browbeaten into doing so, that will only reinforce our sense of self-righteousness.

When we imagine ourselves as the person being shouted at, things look rather different. We all know how unpleasant it is when someone shouts or swears at us. It brings up feelings of resentment, unfairness, or even fear – particularly if we think the shouting might lead to a punch in the face. Remembering how easily we can be hurt in this way should encourage us to avoid all harsh speech ourselves, and to encourage others to do likewise. And when we do inevitably speak harshly to someone, the least we can do is apologize.

Letting go of harsh speech, and developing the habit of speaking softly and courteously – even common politeness – helps to encourage a less aggressive and more gentle approach to others. In the *Metta Sutta* the Buddha reminds us that to be skilled in goodness we need to be 'straightforward and gentle in speech'. This brings together the ideas of speaking with both open honesty and gentleness, rather than from a mind of deception or aggression. By developing this habit, we may be able to become one who 'speaks such words as are gentle, pleasing to the ear, and loveable, as go to the heart, are courteous ... and agreeable to many'.[4]

* * *

The Buddha also warns his followers not to indulge in frivolous, idle or useless talk. Do we really have to be serious all the time? It's enjoyable to play with words and to exploit the flexibility of the English language. But if we're honest, we sometimes speak foolishly and without real meaning, simply chatting or repeating nonsense. We all know how irritating it is when someone is simply prattling on about nothing worthwhile.

This doesn't mean we need to restrict our speech entirely to spiritual matters. That would be a nightmare. Our daily life calls for many necessary conversations to get the shopping done and to put the food on the table – as well as getting the kids to school, sorting out work for the day, and a hundred other things. Conversation can be used to exchange information, to reassure someone or to put them at their ease – or just to have fun.

Perhaps the habit to be aware of here is speaking without purpose, talking for the sake of talking or to avoid the awkward feeling that silence sometimes brings. If we can let go of this habit, we may be more likely to use words wisely – and perhaps more sparingly – speaking when we have something useful or helpful to say. The Buddha encourages us to avoid useless chatter, and also speaking at the wrong time with 'such words as are worthless, unreasonable, immoderate, and unbeneficial'. Instead he encourages us to speak at the appropriate moment with 'such words as are worth recording, reasonable, moderate, and beneficial'.[5] At least we should be aware of what we are saying, and attempt to say only what is sensible. He gives a wise piece of advice about when to remain silent. If what you are about to say is either untrue or unhelpful, keep silent. If it is both true and helpful – wait for the right time!

The Zen Precepts

As well as the Five Precepts common to all schools of Buddhism, the Zen tradition has adapted the Buddha's ten wise and foolish actions to give five further precepts, often relating to our speech and to our mental actions, our patterns of thought. The sixth and seventh Zen precepts deal mainly with skilful speech, though they're phrased differently, which may help us to look at skilful speech from another angle. (We'll catch up with the final three Zen precepts later on in chapter 11.)

The sixth Zen precept is often given as *not speaking against others*, reflecting the Buddha's encouragement to avoid slander and malicious speech – and perhaps harsh or rude speech and gossip as well. Modern Zen versions may be phrased as a directive – *Do not speak against others* – or as a vow or promise – *I will refrain from speaking against others*. Other versions include not slandering others or discussing their faults, or emphasize the positive side of the precept – *I take up the way of speaking of others with openness and possibility*.

It's so easy to join in a conversation about the faults of other people, the negative gossip about people we know, or the general grumbling about everyone from the irritating work colleague to the corrupt politician.

We may not actually be slandering them – their faults may be all too real – but we're certainly not treating them with respect. And blaming them for their inappropriate actions, or perhaps just for being so annoying, allows us to continue safely without taking any action ourselves. *It's their fault, they should do something about it, it's not my job to sort it out.* So again this is partly about *me* being right and blameless. Of course we need to be aware of the mistakes that we and other people make, but our tendency to criticize can easily become what Diane Rizzetto calls 'tinted glasses obscuring a clear view of who or what we meet at any given time'.[6]

It's difficult to listen carefully when we hear someone being criticized, weighing up whether the comment is fair or not. We may tend to criticize others and exaggerate our own virtues, though this is hardly conducive to harmony and well-being. It's hard to maintain a neutral attitude when we have no evidence one way or the other, but even harder to step in and challenge what we know to be a false accusation. We often want to fit in with our group, and the group wants to feel superior to whoever is being criticized. So again this behaviour is often about *me* and my ego, the wish to be accepted, the fear of being isolated if we speak out. Can we let go of that and find a more kindly response, at least refraining from joining in, and maybe eventually finding the courage to challenge unfair criticism?

When we see examples of injustice or cruelty, we may need to speak out rather than remain silent. Reb Anderson suggests we do this 'with a heart that is free of self-concern', to unite rather than divide those who may be listening to us. In this way we can still speak compassionately even when we are pointing out wrongdoing. This sixth precept goes beyond avoiding slander, and invites us to examine our underlying selfish motives. In this way it can help us to 'develop the compassionate and liberating potential of human speech'.[7]

Again we can try to combine positive and negative aspects in the sixth precept, reflecting the Buddha's description of wise and unwise actions:

Letting go of harsh and divisive speech, I take up the way of kindly and gentle speech, the way of promoting concord.

* * *

The seventh precept is sometimes expressed as *Do not be proud of yourself and devalue others.* Other versions include not praising oneself and slandering, reviling, abusing or blaming others. This may be expressed as a vow or promise – *I will refrain from being proud of myself and belittling others* – or more positively – *I take up the way of not praising myself while abusing others.*

If we speak well of ourselves and speak ill of others, or even if we *think* we are better than them, we are again only boosting our selfish ego. This is a form of delusion. Diane Rizzetto suggests investigating this precept to show us how we measure our worth by comparing ourselves with others. This begins with the way we speak, puffing up our own achievements and belittling those of others, so that we may feel inclined to avoid or ignore them. We may wish to assess ourselves 'as lovers, parents, friends, co-workers, even Zen students', separating ourselves from those we see as inferior, to avoid confronting our own feelings of 'unworthiness, vulnerability and fear'.[8]

But if we do the opposite, seeing ourselves as inferior, speaking or thinking as if everyone else is better than us, we're also feeding our delusive thinking. The feeling that *I'm no good* has as much ego in it as *I'm better than you*. They're both about *me* as the centre of things. When we say something foolish or unkind, it doesn't mean we're bad people, it means that like everybody else we're not perfect. If we look closely at what we say and do, we can see how the mind makes up stories about ourselves – stories we don't have to believe.

We're no different from other people, with our complex mix of good and bad qualities, our habitual mix of wise and unwise actions. The Bay Center version of this precept again puts this neatly: *I take up the way of meeting others on equal ground*. We're neither superior nor inferior to people around us, whether they are our family, friends and neighbours, or anyone else. Let's not take ourselves too seriously! Our images of ourselves, either as wonderful and benevolent people or as miserable and unworthy creatures, are only images. They're not real. If we see ourselves as superior or inferior to others we're either exaggerating our importance or ignoring our innate value.

Exploring this precept can help us to be more open and more forgiving towards the mistakes we recognize we've made. Again it seems appropriate to include both negative and positive elements, to remind us of what we're hoping to leave behind, as well as what we aspire towards. So another version of the seventh precept is:

Letting go of praising myself and maliciously blaming others, I take up the way of meeting others on equal ground.

* * *

This is probably the simplest step of the path to explain, but the hardest to carry out. It's so easy to go along with the harsh criticism of others, rather than to steer a conversation in a more positive direction, or at least to say nothing. We can work on this even when we're alone, as our thoughts can be an endless train of inner speech, ready to fuel our prejudices, and to leap out of our mouths as soon as there's someone there to hear us.

Skilful speech goes beyond following the rules. It's good to remember to speak gently and with kindness, but there's something more personal here. In the same way that skilful thinking implies an imaginative and creative approach, skilful speech includes *finding your own voice*. Rather than simply repeating what we've read, or paraphrasing traditional teachings, we need to find words that are genuinely our own. This is one part of becoming independent in the dharma, and so becoming fully ourselves. This underlines how exploring the precepts is more than simply learning which bad habits to let go of and which good practice to adopt in our actions and our speech. Engaging with the precepts is a matter of finding our own path, finding how our unique background and experience can best be used to find our own way forward – which may differ from anyone else's path.

We live in a society very different from that of the Buddha in ancient India, where speech was the only practical form of communication. We can widen out the idea of wise speech to include wise writing, wise emails, and wise use of social media. However we communicate with people, we need to take time to express ourselves compassionately, rather than firing off messages in the heat of the moment. Perhaps watching the news less often might also be helpful here, or at least being aware of how other people's words and pictures are influencing us.

* * *

Having explored both skilful action and skilful speech, there's one more important area to look at before we turn from morality to meditation – how we operate in our working lives, and what we do with our money.

Chapter 8

And What Do *You* Do for a Living?

The third step in the 'morality' section of the eightfold path is *skilful livelihood*. How should we earn our living? And after housing and clothing and feeding ourselves and our family, how should we spend whatever money is left over?

This is a complex area, trying to find work which doesn't harm others, and which hopefully has real worth for ourselves and our community. Western capitalism places great value on both individual wealth and the economic growth of industrialized societies, but often fails to consider the social and environmental impact of this consumerist expansionism. We are part of this process ourselves, since we have to engage with the conditions of the society we live in, whether or not we wish to challenge them. Some people argue that the spiritual life should try to ignore such worldly matters, but the Buddha would not agree. In the *Sigalaka Sutta* he describes how wealth may be lost through foolish behaviour, and gives advice on how employers and employees should behave fairly towards each other, clearly seeing such areas as important.[1]

Skilful livelihood can draw on all the precepts we have looked at so far. To start with, it implies not taking on occupations which harm other people or animals, or which hinder our own spiritual development. Traditionally in Buddhism this has excluded trading in the five areas of weapons, living beings, meat, intoxicants or poison. We're probably not arms dealers or people traffickers, but we might extend this to cover all military activities, livestock farming, brewing and distilling – and the associated planning and IT and distribution work for all these occupations. Then there are supermarket staff and shopkeepers, who may well be trading in meat and alcohol, toy guns and real guns, poison for rats and slugs – and disinfectant to poison germs.

And what do you do for a living? We've all been asked this question at one time or another, and we're conscious of how our reply may be judged. My main work was as an academic librarian, but I like to mention a part-time role as a university lecturer, to sound more impressive and to prop up my ego. (I put *academic* in front of *librarian* for the same reason.) Our working life is often bound up with our image of ourselves, our success or failure in life. A dear friend of mine was a parish priest for many years, and had some difficulty at first adjusting to retirement: being an Anglican vicar was his identity as well as his job.

If we reflect carefully about how we earn our living, we may find aspects of our own work which *do* harm others, either directly or indirectly. Working in higher education, I'm tempted to give myself full marks here. I never killed animals or sold alcohol – but if I eat meat and drink beer or wine, I'm supporting the livelihood of those who do. And of course the *quality* of our work is also important. Our livelihood can hardly be called skilful if we're incompetent at work, out of our depth, or just plain lazy. Many years ago I was briefly a bewildered and decidedly second-rate schoolteacher. So no full marks for me after all.

There's also work which does no harm, but which is useless. Professional gamblers, for example, work for little other than their own gain. And in our media-led culture, how many celebrities or internet influencers are benefitting anyone except themselves? However, we shouldn't define the high moral ground too narrowly here. There's a fuzzy boundary between those whose work we might see as worthless and the genuine entertainers – from comedians to opera singers – who can bring laughter and joy to their audiences.

Any work which genuinely benefits others is worth undertaking, particularly if it equips them with skills, reduces their suffering or promotes their physical, mental or spiritual well-being. The Buddha often praised the skill of artisans such as carpenters or goldsmiths, using their work as an analogy for the skills acquired in the spiritual life – practical know-how rather than merely intellectual understanding. The variety of important roles needed has become even more obvious during the Covid-19 pandemic. We can't all be teachers, doctors or nurses, therapists or meditation teachers – and much useful work of real benefit is poorly paid and viewed as low status. Without people cleaning our streets and offices, collecting our rubbish, and filling the supermarket shelves, we might soon be both filthy and hungry.

In his classic work *Small is Beautiful*, the German-British economist E.F. Schumacher (1911–77) contrasts what he calls a 'Buddhist economics' with the values of modern materialism. If we see work as a chance to develop and use our skills, to reduce our selfishness by engaging with others, and to produce goods and services which bring real benefit, then it can be deeply fulfilling for us, rather than simply a means of gaining enough to live on. Schumacher argues that unemployment not only leads to poverty but also takes away the 'nourishing and enlivening factor of disciplined work'. Economists who claim that unemployment may sometimes be necessary are putting goods before people, which amounts to 'a surrender to the forces of evil'. Modern economics usually measures living standards by the amount of consumption rather than any increase in well-being, and this balance-sheet approach also ignores the crucial difference between using renewable and non-renewable resources.[2]

Of course our work needs to provide the basic needs of shelter, food and clothing, but we would also hope to find a livelihood which gives us a genuine sense of satisfaction, a chance to use our skills and experience creatively. We might also ask how much we really *need*, both financially and in terms of career advancement. There's the danger of burnout if we take on too much, so that wise livelihood includes looking after yourself in your commitment to work. And if we are unemployed or retired, how do we spend our free time? We could look on this as an opportunity to take up new activities – whether that be voluntary work or even a new hobby. We could see skilful livelihood more widely as spending our time wisely, whether or not we're earning money by our activities.

As well as not killing or otherwise harming living beings, we need to avoid all forms of theft or deceit or exploitation, whether financial or sexual. This might exclude working in advertising, if it means promoting useless products, or encouraging delusions through appealing to the vanity of consumers. Instead we hope to take up work which will encourage us to support and protect living beings, to develop generosity, to treat others with respect and dignity, to be truthful and speak with kindness, free from both stinginess and deluded views. That narrows it down quite a bit!

Buddhist teaching doesn't condemn wealth, as long as it's acquired honestly and then used wisely, rather than greedily hoarded or frittered away. The Buddha described *contentment* as the greatest wealth, emphasizing the need to remain calm in the face of both profit and loss. The danger is that the conspicuous wealth of a few is sometimes achieved at the expense of the majority. Poverty fosters a deep resentment which can easily lead to theft and civil unrest. The ideal of finding a middle way between the extremes of poverty and wealth, both as individuals and as a society, emphasizes our connectedness and interdependence – but puts Buddhism at odds with our rampant consumerist culture.

This need not mean opposing a capitalist system of free enterprise, so long as it is fuelled by a wish to benefit society as a whole, rather than by personal greed. But it certainly hints at the need for an equitable distribution of wealth, if this could be achieved without a communist system of state coercion. All governments should seek to eliminate poverty, especially in rich countries where there is plenty to go around; and those of us who are comfortable should be generous to those who are not. We can't all work in wholefood cooperatives, where all the products are good for you and the cleaner is paid the same as the managing director. But we can at least appreciate the common goal in such firms, where all share equally in the firm's success. This contrasts sharply with large supermarket chains, for example, where the CEO routinely receives the salary of three or four hundred workers who fill the shelves.

The Buddha reminds us in the *Metta Sutta* that those who are skilled in goodness should also be 'unburdened with duties, and frugal in their ways'.[3] This doesn't mean either that we should take it easy at work, or that we should live like hermits. But it does suggest that we shouldn't allow our work to overwhelm us, and we shouldn't waste our money once we have earned it. As well as choosing and following useful and beneficial ways of earning a living, skilful livelihood also includes how we support – or choose not to support – the livelihood of others. This is about spending wisely the money which we have earned. What do we spend our money on? What do we invest in?

It's not as simple as it first appears. For example, if we wish to avoid supporting the tobacco and alcohol industries completely, we can't invest in any supermarkets. Pension fund managers may be required to maximize the return on their investments, irrespective of ethical or environmental concerns. They may support tobacco and alcohol firms – or oil companies and arms manufacturers – without consulting their contributors, who may be unable to influence these investment decisions.

This raises the wider question of how we object to unethical behaviour. If we boycott a particular firm – or a particular country – what effect does that have on the people who live and work there? We might hope that poor working conditions would improve if people boycotted a firm's products. But if the profits went down, they might treat their employees even worse. Sanctions against a country with a poor human rights record might affect the oppressed population rather than the ruling elite. If we wish to change the hearts and minds of those who exploit their workers or their citizens, we need to *engage* with them. A boycott may make us feel better on the high moral ground – but does it actually help those who are suffering?

Perhaps a more practical way to try to affect change is to support campaigning organizations which put pressure on supermarkets, pension-fund managers, global companies and governments. Instead of boycotts they can often use the glare of bad publicity to show up these organizations' lack of concern for their employees, their citizens or the environment.

We might also consider whether it's wise to make a profit out of essential services, either by our employment or our investment. If we're part of profit-making in education or in health services, for example, we may be reducing the overall funding available in these vital areas. The same may be true for utilities such as water, gas and electricity. In the housing market, we might consider whether private landlords are providing an essential service to their tenants, or just using their own wealth to make more money. This is not preaching revolutionary socialism, but simply suggesting that we need to reflect carefully on how we earn our living, and what we do with the money we earn. For example, we might choose to find a highly paid job and give more money to charity, or to earn enough to live on and use our spare time for charitable work. We might consider ethical investments or ethical pension funds. But not everyone is in a position to get full marks here.

The Buddha encourages the appropriate use of wealth to bring happiness to as many people as possible. In one discourse he identifies the very best people as those who seek wealth honestly without exploiting others, and are able to enjoy and to share what they have gained, using their wealth 'without being tied to it, uninfatuated with it, not blindly absorbed in it'.[4] That sounds like good advice for us today.

* * *

The last three chapters have tried to emphasize carefully considering what we're doing and saying, as we go about our daily lives at home and at work. Now it's time to look at the final steps on the eightfold path – skilful effort, skilful mindfulness and skilful meditation.

Chapter 9

Focusing on the Present

If we can learn to cultivate skilful action and speech and livelihood, these three elements can have a profound effect on our lives. But there are further areas to be developed at the same time. Chapter 10 will focus on *skilful meditation*, and here we'll consider *skilful mindfulness*, paying attention to what's going on around us, and being fully aware of our speech and actions. How can I focus on the present moment?

* * *

There's an important difference between *skilful mindfulness* in the Buddhist sense and the modern secular mindfulness industry, which tends to emphasize the pursuit of personal well-being and individual happiness. The Buddhist tradition sees mindfulness in the important context of ethical behaviour. That's why we've looked at skilful action, speech and livelihood before considering a mindful practice. And there's also a less obvious step on the eightfold path to look at first, one which supports all the others, and that's *skilful effort*. The Buddha said that wise effort and wise mindfulness revolve around all the other steps on the eightfold path, supporting both our actions and our meditation practice.

Skilful Effort

Of course effort is needed to abandon our habitual foolish actions and speech patterns, and to develop wise actions and speech instead. The paradox of trying hard to let go is familiar to anyone who's struggled to give up their addictions – whether that means a drink or drug habit, an obsession with food or sex, or a less obvious addiction such as criticizing other people all the time. *Skilful effort* (*samma vayama*) as a step on the eightfold path is rather different. Here we're not so much addressing the things we do or say, but rather but how we think – and who we are. Skilful effort is really important: Dogen reminds us to stop fretting about how clever we are, and simply to 'Practise wholeheartedly: your single-minded effort is itself the way.'[1]

This kind of effort doesn't mean just pushing harder. We're not weight-lifters or marathon runners aiming to improve our personal best. As well as *skilful effort*, we might translate *samma vayama* as 'wise resolve', or perhaps courage, or the wise use of our energy, neither being too lazy to act nor pushing so hard that we risk burning ourselves out. A paradoxical phrase often used in Zen is 'effortless effort', which sounds almost impossible. However, if you lie down for a few minutes at the end of a strenuous yoga session, that's the very gentle effort you're making to relax.

The Buddha encourages us in the *Saccavibhanga Sutta* (the Discourse on the Analysis of Truths) to arouse energy, to exert the mind and to strive – with four specific aims in mind: to prevent 'unwholesome states' or negative emotions such as ill-will from arising; to let go of those that have already arisen; to produce instead 'wholesome states' or positive emotions such as loving-kindness; and to cultivate and maintain these positive mental states.[2] If this sounds repetitive and slightly pedantic, it's worth noting that modern psychologists have found these positive emotions not only *reflect* our mental well-being and resilience, but also help to *develop* it, so that we are better able to cope with whatever the future throws at us.

First then, how do we discourage negative emotions from rising up and threatening our peace of mind? They are described in Buddhist texts as 'hindrances' which keep us tied to suffering. These include the familiar greediness and hatred, but also our dullness and drowsiness, our restlessness and worry, and our nagging doubts and fears. One way of tackling them is to focus on what we experience directly through our senses, viewing our thoughts as passing and not permanent. The British author and campaigner for religious liberty Karen Armstrong explains that our feelings of 'rage, fear, hatred and greed' are inherited from ancestors who were fighting for survival. Instead of blaming ourselves for these negative thoughts, we could instead 'quietly but firmly *refuse to identify* with them', perhaps repeating to ourselves the Buddha's comments we have seen already: 'This is not mine; this is not what I really am; this is not my self.'[3] That's being truly compassionate to ourselves. The Buddha was pointing out that we can't control our physical form, our feelings, perceptions, inclinations or consciousness, willing them to be exactly as we wish. This is because each of them is impermanent, subject to change and thus *dukkha* or unsatisfactory, rather than leading to the happiness we seek. Even more important, they don't represent who we truly are, so we don't have to see them as the core of our being. If we're brave enough, we may also choose to discuss our negative emotions with our spiritual friends. We may be surprised and relieved to find that they also experience rage, fear, hatred and greed, and they may well have helpful ideas about how to cope when we feel overwhelmed.

Secondly, we can learn to let go of these negative emotions when they do arise, by choosing which thoughts we decide to ignore and which to follow. If we feed our angry thoughts, running the story of how badly someone has treated us, the anger will only increase. But if we're aware of the danger, if we question the truth of these thoughts, and if we can divert our attention to something else, this will help us relax and allow the negative thoughts to fade. If they persist, we can move our attention to sending loving-kindness to others, and if all else fails we can anchor ourselves by focusing on our breathing, perhaps counting the breaths, with a minute or two of more formal meditation practice. The Buddha describes how it feels to let go of these emotional states: freedom from greed is like paying off a debt; freedom from hatred is like recovering from an illness; freedom from drowsiness is like being released from prison; freedom from worry is like being freed from slavery; and freedom from doubt is like walking safely out of a desert. Each of these freedoms brings deep gladness and joy.[4]

Thirdly, we can encourage more wholesome mental states or positive emotions by *making our minds glad*. We might recall how we helped someone in the past, and the happiness this skilful action brought, or perhaps remember with gratitude how someone was kind to us. This may not come naturally at first, and it's helpful to keep examples in mind for when you need them. They don't have to be heroic or spectacular. (I recall changing a wheel for strangers stuck by the roadside, or my mother sitting me on her knee and patiently teaching me to read.) This helps to bring the mind into a more peaceful state where there's no room for anger because of the gladness we have generated. Developing gratitude is especially effective here, helping us to experience positive emotions and bringing us closer to other people. We can take time to thank people who have been kind to us – either in person, or by contacting them by phone or email, or simply by remembering their kindness and offering them our thanks. It may help to write down the things or the people or the actions for which we are grateful, and as we shall see, gratitude can become an important part of our formal meditation practice.

Finally, we can cultivate and maintain these positive emotions by resolving to follow the precepts – perhaps reading or reciting them to ourselves, using their expression of the qualities we aim to cultivate, rather than the actions we're trying to avoid. We might bring to mind the peace experienced during formal meditation, or perhaps on a retreat, repeating these positive recollections until they become second nature to us. If we feel ourselves slipping back into negative emotions, Henepola Gunaratana's practical suggestions lead us gently from skilful effort into skilful mindfulness. We can usually overcome anger by offering loving-kindness. Deep breathing, walking meditation, or simply washing your face can help to alleviate drowsiness. Restlessness can be overcome by reflecting on calmness or coming back to the breath. And those nagging doubts and fears may disappear if we can let go of speculation and simply focus on the present moment.[5]

Skilful Mindfulness

So we need to be mindful of both what we wish to let go of, and mindful of what we wish to cultivate. By *mindfulness* we usually mean a state of *being aware*, being present, as opposed to being unaware or absent-minded. So we might define mindfulness as simply paying attention to the present moment. We often make judgements about what we experience, labelling things as positive or negative. Mindfulness includes letting go of that tendency to see everything as good or bad – or at least *observing* the process of judgement, so that we're able to step back from it, so that we're not always running the same old story about how bad things are, or even how wonderful they are. So *skilful mindfulness* (*samma sati*) involves paying constant attention to what's going on around us, noticing without commenting, and so being able to observe our thoughts and feelings without being drawn into our habitual reactions.

Another contrast with the modern mindfulness industry is that *skilful mindfulness* involves a close connection with the Buddhist worldview. The more we pay attention to everything around us, the more we can see that things are impermanent, things are not the way we want them to be, and the world does not revolve around me and my personal wishes.

Here's an experiment to illustrate and demonstrate skilful mindfulness. Pick an ordinary activity, and try to carry it out with your full attention. It might be washing up or brushing your teeth. Anything will do, as long as it's fairly routine, rather than something which needs working out in advance. Can you let go of the idea that washing up is boring, and wash up simply to wash up? Can you brush your teeth without thinking about anything else but brushing your teeth? Can you give the activity your whole attention, just observing it as it is?

This is where meditation and mindfulness overlap and complement each other. You're not sitting on your cushion or your meditation bench or a chair, and you're not watching your breathing. It's more like learning a skill, learning to focus your attention. That's the skill we're practising and learning, whether we call it meditation or mindfulness. There's a fuzzy boundary between the two. Mindfulness is always part of meditation, and meditation is one of the ways to cultivate mindfulness. We might think of them as working together as different aspects of developing a more contemplative life – with mindfulness perhaps more active and meditation more tranquil. For the sake of convenience, I'm treating *mindfulness* here as something we do during our daily lives, the simple practice of being aware. We'll look at *formal meditation* in the next chapter as something we do when we *are* sitting on a cushion or a bench or a chair, for a specific period. The distinction between them is a bit artificial, so let's not worry about it too much.

* * *

The Buddha describes 'four foundations of mindfulness' in the *Satipatthana Sutta* (The Discourse on Establishing Mindfulness).[6] He describes these as 'the direct path' towards purifying the mind, overcoming suffering, attaining the way, and realizing nirvana. He is giving a detailed and lengthy explanation to a group of monks here, so perhaps we can interpret the discourse in rather more general terms. This original path is a very long way from the approach of the modern mindfulness industry!

Mindfulness of the body focuses first on the breath, being aware of inhaling and exhaling in the present moment. Of course this is what we do in our formal meditation, but we can also practice it at any time, to bring the mind back to the present moment, especially at times of difficulty. Then attention is paid to the physical sensations in the body, the movement of the body in walking, and the postures of standing, sitting and lying down. We may also reflect dispassionately on the appearance of the body – young and beautiful or old and wrinkled. This can help us to offer compassion and loving-kindness to all beings, who are like us, subject to ageing and sickness.

Mindfulness of feelings includes observing how the pleasant, unpleasant and neutral feelings we experience often spring from our own mental attitude or emotional state, rather than being caused directly by what we see and hear around us. We tend to react instinctively to these feelings, clinging to a pleasant feeling and recoiling from an unpleasant feeling, without realizing that we may be generating them ourselves by our mood. So we can begin to observe and change ourselves, rather than continually blaming other people and our circumstances when we feel miserable. Seeing that all beings have feelings similar to ours, we may become less selfish, and less inclined to hurt them in any way.

Mindfulness of the mind involves observing how these mental attitudes come and go. The mind is always changing – greedy or generous, hateful or loving, foolish or insightful. Watching this process of change helps us let go of our negative emotions. Let's not feed them by retelling the stories about how someone was nasty to us, or how much we want to get hold of new and better possessions.

Mindfulness of mental objects is the most technical of the four sections. The monks are asked to contemplate elements of the Buddha's teaching: the five hindrances of sensual desire, ill will, sloth, restlessness and doubt; the physical form, feelings, perceptions, mental formations and consciousness which make up a human being; the six senses (including the mind) and the objects they perceive; the 'enlightenment factors' of mindfulness, investigation, energy, rapture, tranquillity, concentration and equanimity; and finally the Four Noble Truths, the heart of the Buddha's teaching.

The advice given to monks in ancient India may seem too complex for us today, but the invitation to be aware of all our thoughts is clear enough. These include our greedy, hateful, drowsy and restless thoughts; ideas prompted by everything we perceive with our senses, including the experience of living in a human body; and our mindful, joyous and tranquil thoughts as well. With careful attention to these thoughts we'll be able to see the difference between them, enabling us to let go of those which lead us into more suffering, and to cultivate those which lead us towards happiness.

It doesn't really matter if we call these four elements mindfulness or meditation. It may be convenient to think of this as mindfulness if we are observing our body, feelings and mind as we go about our daily lives, and think of it as meditation if we are sitting silently in a formal meditation period. Ideally our mindfulness should be continuous throughout the day – but let's not beat ourselves up when we are far from mindful.

* * *

If all this sounds too technical and complicated, we might try the simple mindfulness practice recommended by Daizui MacPhillamy.[7] He encourages us to *do one thing at a time*, paying full attention to whatever it is. Each time your mind wanders away, bring it back to what you are doing, over and over and over again. But if your mind keeps wandering off to the same thing again and again, maybe this is not just a distraction – perhaps it's the next one thing you need to look at, again with your whole attention. It's not always easy to work out what is the one best thing to do next. (I write lists to make me feel more organized – but this doesn't actually get any of the tasks done.) Daizui also suggests not attempting this with grim determination all the time. It's a miserable breakfast when you're so focused on the taste and texture of your bowl of cereal that you can't listen to anyone else around the table. But if you're watching TV and scrolling through your email messages and chatting about the news, you probably won't taste the cereal at all.

The contemporary mindfulness movement often interprets mindfulness as simply paying attention to the present moment, but skilful mindfulness as an aspect of the eightfold path has a deeper significance. As well as paying attention to the ebb and flow of daily life, moment by moment, we are encouraged to remember – to keep in mind – our underlying values and skills. This is an ethical element which involves a certain amount of curiosity, investigating situations as we encounter them. It's rather like a doctor or therapist, listening mindfully to what a patient says in the present moment, but at the same time using their medical training to inform the situation. If we rely only on mindfulness of the present moment, we may misinterpret what we see and hear, making hasty judgements which could be unhelpful. If we rely only on mindfulness of our previous experience, we may be limited to standard responses, which again may be inappropriate. But if we can combine these two aspects of mindfulness, we are more likely to respond wisely and sympathetically to each new situation.

Four Boundless States

Mindfulness also involves cultivating the four 'boundless states' of unlimited loving-kindness, compassion, sympathetic joy and equanimity. In the next chapter we'll explore how we can develop these qualities in our formal meditation, but it's important also to be able to cultivate and practice them in our daily lives.

Loving-kindness and compassion both begin with an offering to ourselves – looking after our own body and mind, making sure that we eat well and sleep well, finding that middle way between the strictness of asceticism and the laziness of over-indulgence. We are often told to avoid being selfish, to put others before ourselves. But in offering loving-kindness to all beings, it's good to start with the one living being we're always carrying around with us. If we can't even be kind to ourselves, how can we be kind to others?

It's wise then to extend this loving-kindness in stages, first to those closest to us – parents and partners, children and siblings and friends – looking after them and their needs, and also being prepared to receive kindness from them. This should be relatively easy, though of course it is not always so! Then we might think of a person for whom we have no strong feelings, perhaps serving us in a shop or delivering our mail. If we can see this 'neutral' person as someone who wishes to be happy and to be loved – just as we wish for ourselves and our family – then we can extend feelings of goodwill wider and wider. Even making eye contact with them, smiling and exchanging a few words, perhaps thanking them for their effort, will make this relationship less neutral and more positive.

Can we gradually bring ourselves to offer loving-kindness towards people we find difficult for one reason or another? However hostile they may be, whatever arguments we may have had, they also wish to be happy and to be loved. They're just like us. If we label them as an enemy, someone to avoid, we're being consciously unkind to them – and we're also making the serious mistake of a dualistic choice. I like *these* people and I'll be nice to them: I don't like *those* people so I won't bother with them. I'll only offer loving-kindness to those who *deserve* it, to those who are kind to me. That's not really good enough, is it?

Finally we attempt to offer this loving-kindness and compassion to all beings. This is what the Buddha encourages again and again in the *Metta Sutta*. Those 'skilled in goodness' should include those who are weak or strong, large or small, close by or far away, wishing: 'In gladness and in safety, may all beings be at ease!' Just as a mother protects her only child, 'So with a boundless heart should one cherish all living beings, radiating kindness over the entire world.'[8] As we gradually extend our ability to offer loving-kindness to all beings, the artificial categories we put them into begin to fade away, so that eventually we don't make these distinctions, and we don't see one person as more or less worthy of our offering of loving-kindness. This is our shared experience of being human.

Sympathetic joy is in some ways the most challenging of the four boundless states. It often seems so difficult to join in someone else's happiness, or to be joyful with them in their success. The delight when a young relative passes an exam, or when a colleague gains an important promotion – it seems to be their delight alone. Of course we congratulate them, but are we genuinely happy for them? There may be a twinge of envy here, wishing we had worked harder at school, or wondering if our own promotion will ever come around.

Again perhaps we can begin with ourselves, learning to appreciate our own kind and generous actions, and allowing ourselves to rejoice when we do something good. We can remind ourselves to be happy and grateful for all the good things in our own life, and in the lives of our family and friends. Gradually we may be able to extend this feeling of gratitude and joy to other people, in the same way as extending the loving-kindness to others. We can try to do this each time we meet someone, or even whenever we think of them.

Equanimity is perhaps more a question of looking at the present moment without making a value-judgement about it. What's happening to us may be wonderful and exciting, or unpleasant and even painful – or in the neutral zone in between, which can appear as just boring. But if we can accept this moment just as it is, we can begin to be calm and balanced, gradually steering ourselves away from our habitual emotional reactions, where we want all the happy moments to last forever, and we recoil from anything unpleasant.

This kind of equanimity involves an active mindfulness rather than a passive indifference. The Buddha underlines this with a series of similes: a herdsman watches his cows carefully to keep them away from the crops; a man walks through a crowd with a bowl full of oil balanced on his head; a surgeon uses a probe to extract an arrow from a wound. These actions require a sustained and active attention to the present moment, without being distracted by feelings of boredom or danger or fear. We're so used to reacting either positively or negatively to whatever happens around us – but as we become more aware of how tied up we are with our emotional responses, they can begin to loosen, allowing us to experience a little more peace of mind.

One of the things which keeps us away from the mental balance of equanimity is the stream of negative thoughts which we often experience, particularly about ourselves. We tend to remember unpleasant experiences more readily than happy ones, and so can come to believe that we're unworthy or worthless or incapable or somehow deficient. It's so easy to get into the habit of believing all the random stuff that the mind throws up. I can still blush when I remember embarrassing incidents from years ago, or times when I was unkind to someone, or made a mess of things at work. But these are just thoughts – we don't have to believe them. Even our most firmly held beliefs about ourselves may not be true. They are real enough – there they are in our minds, telling us we're useless, we can't achieve anything, we can't do anything right. But they may not be *true*. We can also choose to think of times when we were kind and sympathetic to someone who was unhappy, or when we accomplished a complex task well.

* * *

When we're suddenly overtaken by an angry thought, it's sometimes all we can do to keep our mouths shut. We want to shout at the person who has annoyed us, or fire off a terse email in response to their unreasonable request. If we use a little mindfulness, we can pause to look at this anger and see it for what it is – an emotion caused by a thought we don't have to believe. We may still be furious, but we can reflect on that experience. *Oh, so this is how it feels to be really angry.* We're not indulging it, and not trying to push it away, but just being with it. Gradually it will fade as we let go of it, and we can rest with a little equanimity.

Another distinction between mindfulness and meditation is what we might call *breadth of focus*. There's often a certain 'one-pointedness' about meditation, while mindfulness can be (and should be) developed anywhere and everywhere. We can simply be aware of what's going on around us, and inside our minds and our bodies. This is a new form of exploration for many of us, really paying attention to what our senses are telling us, and trying to bring a positive and caring attitude to whatever we observe. It can also be part of the creative process, when we bring our whole attention to making music, to painting or drawing, to writing prose or poetry – or equally when we're listening to music, looking at paintings or sculpture, or reading something we enjoy. Even simply engaging in an open and thoughtful conversation with someone can also be an expression of mindfulness.

* * *

But now it's time at last to get onto the cushion – or the bench or the chair – and see what happens when we bring our attention to bear on the formal process of meditation.

Chapter 10

Skilful Meditation

The final step on the eightfold path is often described as Right Concentration (*samma samadhi*), which can be misleading – Dogen says that Zen meditation is *not* learning to concentrate. The Pali *samadhi* could also be translated as 'collectedness', the focus or well-being generated by a peaceful mind, the opposite of being out of focus, with the mind scattered and agitated. Perhaps the simplest way of describing *samma samadhi* is *skilful meditation*. It complements and supports the eightfold path as a whole. Without developing the other aspects of the path, we won't find the peacefulness of *samadhi*, however hard we try. But when we practise these other elements, that peacefulness will begin to emerge naturally.

Meditation is a huge and sometimes mysterious subject which can only be outlined here. I'll try to explain a little about what it is, why we meditate, and how to set up a regular practice. This will focus in turn on the breath, on loving-kindness, on gratitude, and on walking meditation. If you're new to formal meditation, this should give you enough to get you started on your own, though you may also wish to find a group or a teacher. If you're an experienced meditator, please feel free to skip sections that tell you what you already know.

What *Is* Meditation?

The *Concise Oxford Dictionary* defines 'meditate' as to 'focus one's mind for a period of time for spiritual purposes or as a method of relaxation'. That's not a bad place to start. All forms of meditation involve *focusing* the attention in some way. But there's something else going on as well, which we might describe as opening up to a wider awareness – a *letting go* if you like of our everyday thoughts and concerns. So there's a balance to be found here.

The British psychologist and author David Fontana (1934-2010) describes meditation as 'the direct experience of your own mind'. Most of the time we're only aware of the mind's *contents* – the seemingly random thoughts which come and go all the time, our impressions and opinions, the mixture of happy and sad emotions. When we meditate, we try to develop the ability to step aside and look at the mind itself. Gradually the distractions begin to fade into the background, and beneath them we can find 'a calm, clear awareness, a sense of being rather than doing, of tranquillity instead of confusion'.[1]

Sometimes it's hard to sit still and allow the mind to calm down. The nagging thoughts – the ones we don't want to deal with – may pop up again and again, so that meditation may even include negative experiences, both at first and even later on. The Dalai Lama's simple practical advice is invaluable: 'No matter what is going on, never give up!'

Skilful Meditation is traditionally defined in Buddhist teaching as a series of practices to develop both calm and mental clarity. The Buddha explains in the *Samannaphala Sutta* (The Fruit of Contemplative Life) how experienced meditators can enter and remain in increasingly refined mental states, the four *jhanas*, a series of what might be called 'meditative absorptions', becoming full of stillness and peace.[2] These are increasingly deep meditative states, where first thinking and pondering, then delight and joy, then pleasure and pain, all gradually give way to a mindful equanimity. However, Dogen later insists that Zen meditation is *not* done in stages. Despite these different approaches, even the word Zen comes originally from the Pali term *jhana*, as they both simply mean 'meditation'. Stages or no stages – which path to follow here?

Why Meditate?

The gradual approach, aiming for successively deeper levels of meditation, has always put me off. We often begin meditation hoping either to become less miserable, or to gain a measure of wisdom and insight. But both these motivations look towards getting something out of meditation, getting a *result*. Being happier and less deluded certainly sounds like a good idea, but meditation doesn't really work like that. It's not a deal where you do this much meditation – or perhaps this much *quality* meditation – and you feel this much better. That's a recipe for feeling bad about yourself when you can't keep still, or when your mind keeps wandering. And of course it almost always keeps wandering – that's what the mind does!

So why *do* we meditate? What do we want to get out of it? Do we meditate to get from one level to another? Do we meditate in order to *achieve* anything at all?

People begin meditation for many reasons. Some simply want to relax more and reduce the stress of everyday life. Meditation is very fashionable now, and there are claims that it will improve both our physical and our mental health, and make us more creative individuals. The motivation here may be primarily egocentric, hoping it will give us a more peaceful life. Adverts for meditation courses often emphasize how meditation will make us feel better, rather than how it will help us to look dispassionately at ourselves.

The American Tibetan Buddhist nun Pema Chodron (b. 1936) suggests that meditation can develop five specific qualities. Regular meditation brings a *steadfastness* through the simple 'willingness to sit there'. Gradually a *clear seeing* helps us to observe 'the habitual patterns that limit our life', and we can gain the *courage* to sit patiently with our emotional difficulties and life's problems, nurturing our *attention* to the present moment, and being able 'to relax with the unknown'. And meditation helps us develop an attitude of *no big deal*, not taking ourselves too seriously, whether or not our practice brings the deep insight we might long for.[3]

So if we can be more aware of our mind and how it works, we may be able to think more clearly, be more compassionate, and connect better with others and our environment. As well as meditating on our own, meditating with others – sharing silence in a group – can create a valuable energy. Extravagant claims about how mass meditation can transform the world may be fanciful. But if we see things more clearly, we can live life more skilfully. If we change how *we* are in the world, then we may indeed be able to change the world a little by our influence.

David Fontana suggests that meditation is 'a natural state of mind' to which we all have access, and also 'a form of mental spring-cleaning', which can help us face life's difficulties with a calmer mind and an increased ability to concentrate.[4] The physical benefits of meditation may indeed include relaxing more easily, perhaps with reduced blood pressure and a slower heart rate. The body may be better prepared against illness and infection, more able to tolerate pain, and quicker to heal. And meditators are even said to live longer!

We can train the body to do extraordinary things – climb mountains, run marathons, cycle round the world. Our bodies usually do what they're told. We walk across a room or reach out for a book, without consciously giving the body instructions. Our limbs have been trained to perform such tasks. If only our minds were similarly obedient! Try giving your mind instructions – think about this, or stop thinking about that – and it often doesn't want to cooperate at all. Why don't our minds obey us in the same way as our bodies?

Perhaps we could train the mind as well as the body – train it to be more flexible, to focus on one thing at a time, and to remember stuff instead of forgetting it. Train it to avoid being stressed, to get rid of those unpleasant emotions that keep coming up, and to deal better with the anger and sadness we sometimes feel. What would happen if we chose to *nurture* the mind, to care for it, to look after it, as we wish to look after the body? Perhaps *training* isn't the right word – we're not preparing for a competition. Maybe the best reason to meditate is as a form of mental education – *teaching* the mind rather than training it.

Establishing a Meditation Practice

It's good to establish a regular meditation practice, if possible at the same time and place each day. Some people prefer to meditate early in the morning, while others find the evening more appropriate, to fit in with their circumstances and daily routine. Try to avoid meditating straight after a meal. If you're fortunate enough have a room you use only for meditation, and perhaps for yoga as well, it can develop a lovely peaceful atmosphere – but you can meditate in any quiet space. Some meditators like to have an altar with a Buddha image, and to light candles and incense before meditating. Even if you're only able to meditate for a few minutes each day, try to make it a regular practice, so that you get into the habit when your chosen time for meditation comes around. It's good to have a timer of some sort, and maybe build up gradually to twenty or thirty minutes, once or twice a day.

Before we do any meditation, we need to find a stable and comfortable posture. If you're young and slim and flexible, you may try sitting on a cushion in the lotus posture. Please be careful! Most Westerners find this impossible or extremely uncomfortable. If you sit cross-legged in any posture, alternate which leg you fold in first. (I tucked my right leg in first for years and eventually needed a cartilage operation.) As we get older, meditators tend to move from the cushion to a meditation bench or a chair. There's no reason to stay with a cushion if it hurts – except our stubborn pride. Shunryu Suzuki explains reassuringly that 'The only difference is the legs.'[5] Try to keep your back upright if possible, whether supported or not. If we slump back in an easy chair, we'll lose attention and may doze off at some stage. And if we sit too rigidly, the back will tighten up and cause distracting pain.

Try to find a balance between being relaxed and being alert, both comfortable and attentive at the same time. Close your eyes and feel how the body is in the present moment – the physical sensations in your feet and legs, your bottom on the cushion or bench or chair. Move your attention slowly around the body. See if there's any tension in your feet or legs, your hips or your back, your shoulders or arms, your neck or your face. Maybe stretch or shrug or wriggle around a little to relax any tension. Make sure your hands are relaxed, resting in your lap or on your knees. Then sit as still as you can throughout the meditation period you have chosen.

It's helpful to make a conscious effort to let go of everyday thoughts about our family and friends, our finances, our daily routine, and our past behaviour, bringing the mind into the present moment. Dogen's meditation advice is well worth remembering here:

> Take your meditation seat in a quiet room. Wear loose clothing and arrange it neatly. Put aside all activities, all the conscious mind's reflections about good and bad, right and wrong. Rest one hand in the palm of the other. Sit upright with your head and body centred. Sway your body left and right, then breathe in deeply and breathe out fully.[6]

Once we've found a stable meditation posture, released any tension in the body, and put aside our daily concerns, our thoughts and opinions, we're ready to do some meditation.

Breathing Meditation

This is the simplest and most widely used form. We take the breath as our meditation object as it's always with us, always available, and completely neutral, with no thought or meaning or words attached to it. We use the breathing as an anchor to keep the mind steady. Bring your attention to your breathing, simply being aware of breathing in and breathing out, the natural rhythm which connects us with all other living beings. Just breathe normally, with your attention resting on the physical sensation of breathing, in this present moment.

You may wish to focus on wherever the breath feels most prominent. At the nostrils, notice how the air we inhale is slightly cooler, the air we exhale slightly warmer, after passing through our lungs for a few moments. Notice the sensations of the passage of air in the throat, the expansion and contraction of the chest, the rise and fall of the midriff. Some people find counting the breath helpful – inbreath and outbreath as one, inbreath and outbreath as two, and so on. If you lose count, or when you reach ten, go back to one again. Experiment with counting and focusing on where the breath feels prominent, to find what works best for you.

Soon after we sit down, adjust our posture, and give our attention to our breathing, we notice something else instead. A car drives past the window. Someone calls out in the street. There's an itch on your scalp or a twinge in your knee. And then there's the mind – thoughts wander in uninvited. When we tell the mind to stop everything else and focus on the breath – a simple enough instruction – it often doesn't want to do that at all. Instead it reverts to what we might call the mind's default mode, and produces a stream of questions. *How long can you stay in this position? What's for lunch today? Who's that shouting in the street?* Our mind seems to have a mind of its own!

All these are distractions. They're quite natural, they're just what happens. We hear things, we have physical sensations in the body, and we have thoughts. If only they'd go away we could meditate in perfect silence, with the body balanced and the mind completely clear. But such perfection is probably not going to happen, and if it does, it will only be a few seconds or half a minute before the mind pops up with another question, or the knee twinge comes back, or there's a lorry rumbling past outside.

Each time we notice we're distracted by something, we can just see it as a sound, a sensation or a thought, and bring our attention back to the breath. Let the sound of the car remain just a sound, rather than wondering who's driving around so early in the morning. Let that twinge in your knee remain just a twinge, rather than starting to worry if you have injured yourself. And let the thought – whatever it is – just be a thought, rather than following it up with a narrative about shopping lists or meeting your friends later on. Simply bring your attention back to the breath each time, that natural rhythm, breathing in and breathing out.

If the distraction persists, try moving your attention onto it, listening to the sound of the traffic, feeling the sensation of stiffness in your back, observing that nagging thought that just won't go away. Look at each of these carefully, observe how they change, see how they become stronger and then fade away. If your back or your knee really hurts, then adjust your posture – meditation doesn't have to be painful. Don't be too stubborn to move. But do resist the temptation to be drawn into the narrative of your thoughts – things you need to do later in the day, things you're looking forward to, things you want to avoid. Try to set all of these aside for the moment and return your attention to the breathing – again and again and again.

When one of his students reported being disturbed by thoughts and images during meditation, Shunryu Suzuki responded: 'Whatever bird flies through the sky, the sky doesn't care.' That's the way to think of your thoughts! On another occasion he suggested we shouldn't try to blot out our thoughts in meditation: 'Leave your front door open and your back door open. Let thoughts come and go. Just don't serve them tea.'[7]

* * *

When the bell on your timer rings, move slowly and calmly. Gently open your eyes and perhaps have a little stretch. If you experienced a calmness during your meditation, keep that in mind as you stand up and move around. See if that calmness can carry over and influence the rest of your day.

Loving-Kindness Meditation

We've seen how the Buddha advised us to extend loving-kindness to all living beings, large or small, near or far, and to cherish them in the same way as a mother protects her only child. He concludes the *Metta Sutta* by describing this practice as 'Radiating kindness over the entire world: spreading upwards to the skies and downwards to the depths, outwards and unbounded, freed from hatred and ill-will.'[8] This can be used as a specific meditation practice, taking loving-kindness rather than the breath as our meditation object. Practised regularly, it can be both a powerful antidote to our feelings of fear and isolation, and a method of developing compassion – opening the compassionate heart.

We begin as before by finding a comfortable posture, neither slouching or tense, a balance which is both relaxed and alert. The anchor this time, instead of our breathing, is a succession of short phrases we repeat silently. First we bring our attention gently to ourselves. This is not analysing or judging ourselves, or thinking about our opinions, our likes and dislikes, but simply seeing ourselves as living beings, alive and breathing. Wishing ourselves well, we repeat these phrases slowly, in time with the rhythm of our breathing:

> May I be safe
> May I be well
> May I be peaceful
> May I be happy

As with the breathing meditation, we simply come back to these phrases each time we find ourselves distracted by thoughts or sounds or sensations. If the phrases don't feel appropriate, change the words around until they seem to fit. If this doesn't work, we can focus on the experience itself, asking ourselves how it feels to be safe, how it feels to be well, to be peaceful, and to be happy, in this present moment.

Next we move our attention to those closest to us, our family and friends, offering them our kindness and generosity. We may focus on one or two particular people, or if there is time we can think about each of them in turn – our spouse or partner, our parents and our children, our siblings and their relatives, our close friends and those we see less often. As well as being our family and friends, they're all human beings just like us, living and breathing and wishing to be happy. So we take some time wishing them well, repeating the phrases:

> May you be safe
> May you be well
> May you be peaceful
> May you be happy

Then we move our attention to someone for whom we have no strong feelings. We perhaps only see them occasionally and hardly notice them – we might even be indifferent to them. This could be someone who delivers our mail, or who checks out our shopping at the supermarket. And again they are just like us, human beings who suffer and who long for happiness. So again we wish them well, repeating the same phrases:

> May you be safe
> May you be well
> May you be peaceful
> May you be happy

If we feel able to do so, we can include next anyone we have found difficult. This might be an awkward colleague or an argumentative neighbour. We may feel tempted to ignore these people, or to blame them for the difficulties they have caused us. But of course they are living and breathing human beings just like us, people who suffer and who wish to be happy. Can we set aside any ill-feeling we have towards them and instead wish them well?

> May you be safe
> May you be well
> May you be peaceful
> May you be happy

Gradually we can try to extend our loving-kindness to the whole of life, as the Buddha recommends: 'Radiating kindness over the entire world ... outwards and unbounded'.[9] We might think first of our own community, our neighbours – even the awkward ones – and then maybe our whole county or state. We can offer loving-kindness to all those who live in the country we live in – and then to other countries, and even those in other continents. Although we've never met them, we know that they are like us, human beings who suffer and who long for happiness. We may eventually be able to reach out beyond our human family to other animals, to our cats and dogs, to the birds of the air and the fish in the sea. Can we even extend this loving-kindness to trees and plants? Eventually we can wish the whole of life well, using similar phrases:

> May all beings be well
> May all beings be peaceful
> May all beings be happy

Finally we come back to ourselves, the person who is expressing these wishes, reminding ourselves that we are connected to all other living beings, hurtling through space on this ball of rock we call the Earth. So we can end this meditation by again wishing ourselves well:

> May I be safe
> May I be well
> May I be peaceful
> May I be happy

As before, when the bell on your timer rings, move slowly and calmly. Gently open your eyes and perhaps have a little stretch. If you experienced a calmness during your meditation, keep that in mind as you stand up and move around. See if that calmness can carry over and influence the rest of your day.

Gratitude Meditation

Even when we're not feeling peaceful and happy, when it's difficult to project these positive feelings towards those around us, we still have much to be grateful for. We have a precious human life, food and shelter, education and health care – and we have the capacity to reflect, to be aware of the present moment, and to be aware of other people, whose life is just as precious to them. We tend to take for granted our home, with its water and electricity supply, our schools and hospitals – but these are all reasons to be grateful. A large proportion of the human family don't have the benefits we enjoy. A great many people have been involved in providing us with all these good things, supporting our comfortable life.

Gratitude meditation can help us to notice more often what we should be grateful for, and so to experience more positive thoughts, rather than grumbling all the time. This meditation leads our thoughts away from our own selfish concerns and connects us more intimately to others, whose lives are just as precious. This practice allows us to experience our connection with other people and with all life, helping us to cultivate generosity, and it may also help us to forgive anyone who has harmed us.

We begin as before by finding a comfortable posture, neither slouching or tense, a balance which is both relaxed and alert. As with the loving-kindness meditation, we can use simple phrases to express our gratitude. Those given below are just an example. You may wish to experiment with them to find the most suitable phrases for different groups of people, again repeating them silently and slowly in time with the rhythm of your breathing.

We may choose to begin with our parents, thinking of all they did for us – giving us this precious human life, teaching us to walk and to feed ourselves, giving us food and shelter, keeping us safe, setting us off to school, and a great deal more. I always find this a moving and helpful meditation, worth practising regularly and at some length. Like many people, I had an awkward relationship with my parents as a teenager, and I was not able to show my gratitude for all their efforts and kindness before they died. Whether they are still alive or not, think of all your parents did for you over the years:

> I treasure your efforts
> I cherish your kindness
> I am grateful for your existence

Next we move our attention to our friends and family, for all those who have supported us throughout our lives. If you have time, think of each of them in turn, remembering their kindness towards you, giving you their friendship, their helpful advice and their time. As with the loving-kindness meditation, we remember that they are living and breathing human beings just like us, who long for happiness just as we do:

> I treasure your efforts
> I cherish your kindness
> I am grateful for your existence

Then we think of the many people who have supported our present comfortable life, providing us with food and shelter, water and electricity, education and health care. We've probably never met most of them – the farmers and banana growers, the builders and plumbers and electricians – and we may feel indifferent to those we have met – fixing a leaky pipe or mending our roof – but each of them has used their training and expertise to make our lives more comfortable. And like us, each of them longs for happiness:

> I treasure your efforts
> I value your skill
> I am grateful for your existence

Next we can bring our attention to our dharma teachers and dharma friends, those who have inspired or guided or supported any aspect of our spiritual life. Think of the people who first introduced you to your tradition – whether you still follow it or not – and those who have guided you along the way, or whom you think of as a spiritual friend. These may be people you see every week in a meditation group, or teachers whose writings have inspired you, even if you've never met them:

> I treasure your efforts
> I cherish your understanding
> I am grateful for your existence

To end this meditation, we can come back to ourselves again, remembering how fortunate we are to be here in this present moment, making the effort to be grateful, understanding how others deserve our gratitude, and having the many benefits of our precious human life:

> I treasure this effort
> I cherish this understanding
> I am grateful for this existence

You may find it helpful to make these phrases less personal, taking the 'I' out and simply repeating:

> Treasuring your efforts
> Cherishing your kindness (or your skill or understanding)
> Grateful for your existence

Again as before, when the bell on your timer rings, move slowly and calmly. Gently open your eyes and perhaps have a little stretch. If you experienced a calmness during your meditation, keep that in mind as you stand up and move around. See if that calmness can carry over and influence the rest of your day.

Walking Meditation

We usually think of meditation as a sitting-down practice, whether on a cushion or bench or chair. But in the *Metta Sutta* the Buddha says: 'Whether standing or walking, seated or lying down, free from drowsiness, one should sustain this recollection'.[10] The recollection here is that of radiating loving-kindness, but the point is well made. We can meditate while standing or even while lying down – as long as we remain free from drowsiness. But the usual alternative to seated meditation is walking meditation. This is extremely useful if we are sitting for long periods, perhaps on retreat, or if we find sitting uncomfortable. In our Zen group we have two periods of sitting meditation, with ten minutes walking meditation in the middle. We walk slowly in a circle, but it's just as helpful to do some walking meditation on your own.

Stand up slowly from your seated meditation, and find a space to walk. Try walking up and down in a line with maybe twelve steps each way, and small steps to turn around, in time with the rhythm of your breathing. In this way we can maintain the breath as part of the meditation. But we also focus on the physical sensation of moving. Again this is simply to anchor the mind, watching the body as each leg lifts and moves forward and takes the weight again. Sometimes meditators are encouraged to walk extremely slowly, thinking *lifting, lifting, moving, moving, placing, placing*, but you may find this distracting. Your focus may soon shift to not wobbling or falling over! So walk slowly but not too slowly, letting your attention rest on the combined rhythm of walking and breathing. After a few minutes any stiffness in your legs or your back has probably eased, and if you wish you can return to your seated meditation.

Great Expectations

If we can establish a regular practice, perhaps combining some or all of the meditations described above, we may expect things to happen. Some people report mystical experiences, some feel an overwhelming sense of peace, and some may feel that there is actually nobody there meditating, only a sense of complete awareness. Then the thought pops up: *I'm really doing this right, I'm a good meditator.* And of course that thought breaks the spell and the moment is gone.

Other people meditate regularly for years, and little or none of this happens. Even when we're in a comfortable and stable posture, and the traffic is quiet, the mind will set to work trying to make a story out of any random thought that comes along, or the slightest sensation in the body. Off we go! Is that just a twinge I can feel? No, the back pain seems a little worse today. Should I give up this meditation bench and retreat to sitting in a chair? It would be easier if I lost some weight. Shall I go out for a bike ride? I should have checked the weather ... and so on and on.

After a moment or two - or perhaps a minute or two - we catch ourselves making up these stories and questions, and bring our attention back to the breath or the loving-kindness meditation. There's no need to beat ourselves up about this, as it's simply the mind wandering. That's what the mind often does. When the thought comes in that we're bad meditators, just treat it as another thought. It's a real thought, it exists - but it's not true. It's just another distraction to let go of.

Even when we've built up our meditation session to half an hour, the same thirty minutes will seem quite short one day, and almost endless the next day. This will depend on whether you're tired or not, what has happened during the day if you're meditating in the evening, how much you have had to eat and how well you have slept. One day the timer will go off after what feels like a few minutes, and the next day you'll think the timer has broken and you've been sitting there forever.

So don't worry about whether your meditation seems to be good or bad. We're not doing it to get somewhere else, to gain some merit marks or to get up to the next level of anything. If you sometimes get fed up with meditation, just keep on going, and don't worry about that feeling of dissatisfaction. It's just another distraction. If we start to give up and let our regular practice lapse - that's when our mood changes and we begin to feel less happy, more irritable or more fearful. These feelings remind us why we're meditating!

* * *

The eightfold path is often portrayed as an eight-spoked wheel in Buddhist iconography, reminding us that each step supports all the others. We've considered them here in sequence, from skilful view to skilful meditation, as it would be confusing to read about all eight at once. But in our spiritual practice that's exactly what we have to do. We can't work our way through one by one, ticking them off the list when we think we've made enough progress. If this sounds a bit like keeping all the plates spinning at once, or juggling to keep all the balls in the air, there's no need to worry. If we're aware that a spiritual life is worthwhile, if we're developing ethical behaviour and loving-kindness, and if we're practising meditation on the cushion and mindfulness away from it, all that just might begin to lead us towards wisdom.

Chapter 11

A Path towards Wisdom?

What do we mean by wisdom – and how do we reach out towards it? We can often recognize a wise person when we meet one, or a wise comment when we read one. But what is it that we recognize? T.S. Eliot expresses an important distinction when he asks: 'Where is the wisdom we have lost in knowledge?'[1] This reminds me of long lessons at school, learning more and more factual information to pass increasingly difficult exams – acquiring lots and lots of knowledge, but precious little wisdom.

The most commonly used Buddhist term for wisdom is *prajna* (pronounced *prajnya*). In a sense this is what Buddhist teaching is all about – the conclusion of the eightfold path. But it's not merely *knowing about* something – it's more an *awakening* than an accumulation of knowledge. That's the difference between reading about the Buddha's teaching and practising it, experiencing it for ourselves. When we're young, we think we're going to live forever, and our understanding of impermanence is very limited. As we grow older, our body slows down and may need repairs to keep it going. So we begin to experience for ourselves what change and impermanence is all about.

Prajna is variously described as insight or 'discriminating knowledge', or perhaps 'intuitive apprehension'. The term *prajnaparamita* – the *perfection* of wisdom or insight – is close to being the same as awakening or enlightenment. The *Prajnaparamita Sutras* – including the *Heart Sutra* and *Diamond Sutra* – are seen in the Mahayana tradition as the ultimate expression of wisdom literature. These texts refer again and again to what has been called a 'transformative wisdom' which by its nature prompts skilful and generous behaviour directed to all beings. This is the 'compassion in action' exemplified by the perfection of wisdom.

Skilful Understanding and Skilful Thinking

So is wisdom the end of the path, the goal, something we reach *after* practising morality and meditation? Well, yes and no. If wisdom is marked by skilful understanding and skilful thinking, we started out with at least a little of each.

This skilful understanding – the wise perspective – which we took on trust as we set out on the eightfold path, is eventually confirmed by our experience. We learn for ourselves that actions really do have consequences for good or ill, and that the spiritual life is indeed worth undertaking. As we practise the four tasks of understanding and accepting unsatisfactoriness, letting go of our habitual reactions, observing how these reactions can fade, and cultivating the eightfold path, we begin to experience how our behaviour and our attitudes can change. The ten wise actions, prompted by generosity, loving-kindness and insight, and reflected in the Zen precepts, are no longer simply a list of things we need to do. Hopefully they have become part of our physical and mental make-up – part of who we are. The characteristics of unsatisfactoriness, impermanence and the lack of a permanent fixed self are no longer simply how we describe the Buddhist worldview. They are at last something we've genuinely experienced for ourselves, rather than something we've read about, or something we've chosen to believe as a doctrine.

Similarly, the skilful thinking – the wise intention or wise resolve – which we again initially took on trust, is gradually confirmed by the experience of our practice. Letting go of our unhelpful mental habits, offering loving-kindness and compassion to all living beings, cherishing them all equally, and learning to examine our actions, thoughts and emotions – all this slowly brings into effect what that wise monk suggested long ago – you can indeed *change your mind*. Skilful thinking may also eventually include cultivating new ways of thinking, guided by our reading and practice, with a willingness to engage with what Daizui MacPhillamy calls 'honest questioning' and 'constructive doubt'.[2]

One of these new ways of thinking is what we might call a more *creative* approach. Following fixed ethical rules is easier and less complex than looking at each situation in turn, and then acting on what we feel in our hearts rather than what the texts tell us to do. Our habitual reactions can stifle our creative ability to take risks, to make use of our imagination.

The creative arts have played an important role in Buddhist countries, from Thai temple paintings to Tibetan ceremonial music. In the Japanese tradition, Zen artists have expressed the immediacy of their experience in painting, calligraphy, poetry, and monastic buildings and their gardens. Although there is little about creativity in the original Pali texts, a few passages do hint at a creative and imaginative role. In the parable of the city, for example, the Buddha imagines a man who finds an ancient path, leading through a forest to a ruined city.[3] He reports this discovery and the city is restored, becoming once more inhabited and prosperous. The man in the forest is the Buddha himself, and the ancient path is the eightfold path, which the Buddha has rediscovered, rather than invented for himself. The image of the restored city strongly suggests that the end of the path is not so much enlightenment for the individual, but more what Stephen Batchelor calls 'a space that encourages human flourishing', a place where 'residents build a communal and social future' – a new *society*, rather than a new religion.[4]

As we have seen, the Buddha also admires the skill of the artisan – the potter, the ivory-carver or the goldsmith – who can transform raw material into useful or beautiful objects. He compares these processes with the skilful practitioner whose mind is similarly purified and cleansed, easily controlled, 'malleable ... pliant and properly concentrated'.[5] The implication is that our whole body-mind can be seen as the raw material, capable of being transformed into the awakened person we might be – if we have both the skill and the perseverance.

This reminds us that the Pali term *sankappa* – usually given as *thought* or *intention* in the second step on the eightfold path – could also be translated as imagining or planning. So *samma sankappa* could be seen as *skilful imagination* or even *skilful creativity*. This would fit well with the idea of the path as something to be *cultivated*, to be brought into being, to be created – a path made by walking.

If we can let go of our opinions, our fears and judgements, and observe carefully and dispassionately what our senses tell us, we may be more open to seeing each situation clearly, and then acting accordingly. Letting go of the wish to be in control needs both honesty and courage. Always knowing what to do sets up a standard where we judge ourselves and will always fall short. Instead, *not* knowing what to do next may actually be an aspect of wisdom – the wisdom to trust what our heart tells us, rather than to follow any set of rules.

The Mountain of Wisdom

Our skilful imagination might conjure up a picture of wisdom as a mountain, with an invitation to ascend to the summit. There are many paths on this mountain of wisdom. Some are long and winding but fairly gentle, others are more direct but fearsomely steep. At any point at the foot of the mountain we can't see which paths lead to the summit, or merge with other paths, or peter out halfway up. We can't see anything of the paths leading up from the foothills elsewhere beneath the mountain – the Jewish or Christian or Muslim paths, the Hindu or Sikh paths, or any number of other paths completely unknown to us. So we might be wise to remain silent about where the other paths do or don't lead.

Several paths lead upward from our own particular foothills, which we might call the Buddhist side of the mountain (including the partly Buddhist, not-just-Buddhist, or Buddhist-leaning foothills). There's a tourist path of secular mindfulness which winds gently out of sight around the corner, perhaps only leading to a plateau rather than onwards up to the summit. There are several monastic paths, which all look too steep for the vast majority of us. Then there's a Theravada path, a Tibetan path and a Zen path – or rather a series of broader or narrower paths in each tradition. Each of them has its own attractions, and each path probably has tricky sections to negotiate higher up. Or you might choose to look for your own path leading between them – a path made by your own feet, a path made by walking.

My first glimpse of this mountain came as a child, when I was taken to meet my grandfather, a retired Methodist minister. This elderly gentleman sat in an armchair, beaming at his youngest grandson. I remember feeling pleasantly confused. His presence filled the whole room with something I had never encountered before – something positive and powerful which could neither be seen or heard. It was many years before I realized that this invisible substance was *wisdom*.

I remember, as a teenager, looking down at the sea from a clifftop path one evening. I saw for a magical minute or two that the rocks and the water, the sky beyond and the setting sun, and the boy watching them, were not different objects but part of the same whole. Again it was years later before I recognized this as a falling away of the sense of separation, the feeling of being *in here* looking at *things out there*. For just that minute, there was no *in here* and *out there* as separate entities. And again, this looks like the beginning of wisdom.

The Wisdom of Generosity

The final three Zen precepts relate to the three mental actions in the Buddha's list of wise and foolish actions. They're phrased in the same way as the others, but there's a sense in which these are not so much *moral* precepts, but more *wisdom* precepts. They seem to reflect a more profound letting go of our familiar greed, hate and delusion, replacing them with a wise and all-encompassing generosity, loving-kindness, and insight.

The first of these is meanness or stinginess, or just plain greediness. The Buddha encourages us not to covet anyone's wealth or property, wishing it was all ours, to avoid all such greed and to develop instead generosity, contentment and tranquillity. So the most direct form of the eighth precept is: *Do not be mean in giving dharma or wealth*. Elsewhere it is expressed as refraining from giving spiritual or material aid grudgingly and giving it freely where it is needed – always being generous instead of being stingy.

Of course we need to find skilful ways to discover and to offer what is needed. Being generous benefits those who receive our generosity, but it also changes us, and changes our relationship with other people. By learning how to give, we also learn how to accept, how to receive kindness and generosity from those who offer it to us.

Reb Anderson advises us to become familiar with offering our possessions and our time to others. We can even help to give them *fearlessness*, by fostering their self-respect and confidence. And we can offer them the precious gift of the dharma – not as formal teachers, but simply by offering whatever is most helpful to them, asking ourselves: 'What is the most precious thing that I can give right now?'[6] The underlying attitude is not being possessive, either by hoarding possessions while others have little or nothing, or by jealously keeping the Buddha's teaching to ourselves. We should be willing to share both material possessions and the dharma freely with others.

It's so easy to allow our thoughts to become focused on the things we want, or the attractive things other people have. These mental actions of greed or covetousness or jealousy are particularly unwise, and can lead to intense frustration about not having what we want.

Again the positive aspects of the precept encourage us to think instead with a mind of generosity and contentment. As before, we can attempt to combine the positive and negative aspects of the eighth precept:

> *Letting go of stinginess, I take up the way of freely offering spiritual or material help to all those who are in need.*

The Wisdom of Compassion

The Buddha encourages us again and again to avoid all hate or ill-will, and to generate thoughts of goodwill, and so to develop compassion. Expressed as a directive, this ninth precept is phrased: *Do not be angry*, which can be misleading. It implies that being angry is wrong, so if angry thoughts come into our mind, we have failed to keep the precept. But as we know, both pleasant and unpleasant thoughts pop into our minds unbidden all the time, whether we like it or not. We're responsible for how we react to these thoughts, wisely or foolishly – but not for the thoughts themselves. It's simply not realistic to forbid anger, to avoid anger, or to promise never to become angry. This isn't the way the human mind works. It's more that we shouldn't *indulge* anger, or *harbour* anger and ill-will in our minds. A harbour is place of shelter where boats are safe from the open sea. So if we harbour anger, we're allowing it to drop anchor in our minds and rest there securely.

The Chinese version of the Mahayana *Brahmajala Sutra* (The Brahma's Net Sutra) gives this precept the title: *On feeding anger and hardheartedness*, and advises us neither to maintain anger against someone, nor to encourage others to do so. It's not so much the arising of anger which is the problem, but the temptation to feed this ill-will, to maintain our hard-hearted feelings, rather than allowing them to subside. So a more helpful phrasing may be: *I will refrain from indulging anger*, or again, more positively: *I take up the way of letting go of anger*.

When a driver pulls out in front of you, causing you to swerve or brake sharply, there's a rush of adrenalin, and rude words may well escape from your mouth. That flare-up of anger is usually over in a few seconds. Off he goes, no harm done. The danger is when we keep the flame burning, chasing the culprit and trying to catch up, flashing our lights and leaning on the horn. That's *road rage*, where harbouring anger can lead to a shouting match or even a violent confrontation.

Diane Rizzetto suggests that this precept is not about *denying* anger, believing that it's always wrong, always to be avoided – which we can't do anyway – but rather *understanding* anger, observing it carefully when it arises. Then we can begin to see the difference between the familiar anger driven by our ego – the frustration of me not getting what I want

– and what she calls 'life-centred anger, anger that is a genuine response to support life'. Any anger which prompts us to harm ourselves or others is almost certainly a self-indulgent, ego-driven emotional response. But a life-centred anger prompts actions which can benefit ourselves or others: it can be 'open and transformative ... filled with potential for useful action'.[7] So if we're seething about an injustice or the unfair treatment of someone, we can do something positive – join a campaign group, write letters, offer practical help to whoever is suffering. If we can do this with a positive wish to make the situation better, to overturn the injustice or to reduce the suffering, then our anger will not have been worthless.

Sometimes our anger is just an overwhelming blind rage. That's when we need to take action to divert our attention from it, by simply doing something else. Count your breaths, go for a walk, take a shower, listen to your favourite music. Whatever works for you. Gradually the anger will settle down, and we can begin to observe it, to see that it was probably prompted by something very familiar – *dukkha* or 'unsatisfactoriness'. Either we didn't get what we wanted, or we had to endure something we didn't want. It happens all the time.

If we can learn to let go of our ego-driven anger, and to channel our life-centred anger into positive action that will help others, then instead of harbouring anger, we'll be able to experience instead a measure of compassion, where we are able to generate thoughts of goodwill and loving-kindness.

Again we can combine the positive and negative aspects of the ninth precept:

Letting go of harbouring anger and ill-will, I take up the way of compassion, offering goodwill and friendship to all living beings.

The Wisdom of Insight

By now our experience should have confirmed much of what we originally took on trust. If we ever thought that actions have no consequences, and there's no point to the spiritual life, we wouldn't have set out on the eightfold path in the first place. Reflecting on our behaviour and continuing our mindfulness and meditation practice, we've hopefully understood more about actions and their results, and increasingly realized the value of the spiritual life. This is skilful understanding or wise view.

The tenth and final Zen precept again reflects the Buddha's exhortation to avoid deluded or false views, and instead to think clearly and so develop insight and wisdom. It's been changed almost beyond recognition as the Buddha's teaching has developed. The precept is now often expressed as: *Do not defame the Three Treasures*. Elsewhere this is variously given as not to revile or disparage or slander the three jewels – the Buddha, the Dharma and the Sangha – but instead to cherish and uphold them.

Certainly Zen practitioners would wish to honour and respect the three treasures. Why would they need to be told not to berate the Buddha, disparage the Dharma, or slander the Sangha? I can't help thinking that the original intention – to avoid the foolish mental action of wrongheaded views, and instead to develop insight – has been hidden within with the much narrower verbal action of slandering the Buddha, the Dharma or the Sangha.

Do not defame the Three Treasures might be seen as a Buddhist version of the Old Testament commandment: *Do not take the Lord's name in vain*. It has the same tone of religious authority, warning us to avoid undefined wrongdoing, rather than encouraging us to develop wisdom. I prefer the Buddha's original idea of wise and foolish mental actions – not demanding orthodoxy, but encouraging people to give up their delusive thinking, and to develop clear insight which can lead to wisdom.

Perhaps there's a middle way between these different versions. In taking refuge in *buddha* (rather than *the Buddha* as an individual person), we're acknowledging the awakened potential of all beings. In taking refuge in *dharma* (rather than *the Dharma* as the Buddha's exclusive teaching), we're entering the wide ocean of wisdom and compassion. In taking refuge in *sangha* (rather than *the Sangha* as the Buddhist monastic community), we're recognizing the interdependence of all beings, not just those with spiritual authority. If we deny people's spiritual potential, or turn our backs on wisdom and compassion, or ignore the interdependence of all beings – we're certainly harbouring false views, but we're also denying the reality of buddha, dharma and sangha. The three treasures are not just Gotama and his teaching and a group of monks and nuns. The three treasures are also our spiritual potential, our wisdom and compassion, and our dependence on one another. If we deny these we can only be ruled by their opposites, the familiar poisons of greed, hatred and ignorance. But if we cherish them, we will also be cultivating generosity, loving-kindness and insight.

False views are as much a failure of the imagination as anything else, a failure to appreciate things as they really are. The interdependence of all beings, for example, is a fine-sounding phrase, but what does it mean in practice? The breakfast table gives us a good example. When you next start the day with a bowl of muesli, have a good look before you tuck in. Your favourite mix may include nuts and dried fruit as well as oats and wheat, and you might add a sliced banana before pouring the milk on. So you've been round the world already, with South American and Caribbean farmers and growers, arable and dairy farmers in your own country – and their cows too. Without all these living beings, you'd have to grow all your own food. And someone made your bowl and spoon and milk jug, your chair and table, the room you're sitting in, the bed you slept in – and your house and your street, and the vehicle that takes you to work. Potters and carpenters, house builders and car workers – we really are all dependent on each other, whether we meet up or not.

Again we can attempt to combine the positive and negative aspects of the tenth precept:

Letting go of false views, I take up the way of honouring and respecting buddha, dharma and sangha, the way of cultivating wisdom.

* * *

Trevor Ling – who may very well have been an unofficial Buddhist himself – argued that the Buddhist path is 'essentially a therapy', but not for curing the individual, since 'individualism is the disease for which a cure is needed'. The very object of Buddhist morality is to erode the persistent belief in 'one's own permanent individuality'. So the wisdom which is finally arrived at, after practising morality and meditation, is essentially our 'liberation from the state of being bound to the ego-idea'.[8]

After exploring and following the precepts, practising daily meditation, and developing compassionate behaviour, the fourth pillar of Zen practice is *realizing* – making real rather than merely understanding – our 'Buddha nature'. This is surely what D.T. Suzuki meant by our essential 'inner purity and goodness', and what Philip Kapleau called our 'original perfection'. It's also the freedom from that persistent idea that *getting what I want* is the most important thing. Letting go of the wanting, and letting go of the *me* who does the wanting – this is the spiritual wisdom of awakening.

Chapter 12

All Together Now

So far, we've been discussing the different aspects of the eightfold path mainly from the perspective of an individual practitioner. Of course this often involves our relationships with other people – we try to be kind and generous, to be honest in our dealings, to enjoy friendly and helpful conversations, and to wish others well in our loving-kindness or gratitude meditation. Even so, practising on our own can be lonely at times, and it can also be difficult to see our practice as a whole, instead of focusing on the individual steps which make up the eightfold path. This leaves us with two final questions. How should we engage with others in our practice? How should we put all these elements of our practice together?

Practising with Others

The Pali term *sangha* usually refers to the Buddhist monastic order, and is still defined as such in dictionaries. But the word simply means 'community'. Even in the Buddha's time there was a 'fourfold sangha' composed of monks and nuns, laymen and laywomen. In modern Western usage, the term has been broadened to describe any group of Buddhists. Practising with others is hugely beneficial, in terms of mutual support and being able to learn from each other. Those of us who meditate regularly at home on our own and also in a meditation group – whether this is a Buddhist group or not – are immediately aware of the difference between these two contexts.

At the most basic level, when we're meditating at home and the niggling back pain returns – or if we just get bored – we can always get up and do something else. Nobody will know. But in the meditation group there's a gentle peer pressure which keeps everyone sitting on the cushion or bench or chair until the bell goes for the end of the session. And there's something else going on here as well, which we might describe as *interdependence*. During the Covid-19 lockdown period, for example, I was meditating frequently with two groups of people – my regular Zen friends and a secular group – but online rather than in person. There were people I had never met in the secular group, but there was the same sense of mutual support and friendship, knowing we all had the same wish to share the silence.

It's really helpful to find a group of like-minded people to practise together. I've been fortunate here for many years, first as part of a Theravada group, then a Zen group, and more recently an unofficial Buddhist group as well. We're a small gathering of spiritual friends who've chosen to share our meditation together, and to discuss our practice. When we're confident enough to share our individual hopes and fears with each other, this has been particularly valuable for all of us.

If you've begun to follow the path of morality, meditation and wisdom on your own, how can you begin to practise with others? First of all, try visiting your local Buddhist lay group or monastic centre. They will almost certainly welcome you as a visitor, whether or not you're familiar with their Theravada, Tibetan, Zen or Western tradition. You may find you have many things in common, and that regular meditation with them – maybe even going on retreat with them – is highly beneficial, even if you're not completely comfortable with all their teaching or their ritual practice. It's very rare indeed (though sadly not impossible) that someone at a centre will tell you that theirs is the only true Buddhism, and only their teaching and practice is valid. If this happens, please feel free to head for the door.

If you're practising in the Christian tradition, see if you can find anyone in your own church or in a nearby congregation who's interested in meditation. You may be surprised! It's just possible that your clergy or church leaders might think this is dangerous and unorthodox. This may be your opportunity to remind them gently of the medieval Christian mystical tradition – or perhaps to look for another church.

You can probably find an online community which supports like-minded practitioners, whether Buddhist or Christian or secular. Most of us are more used to online meetings now, and although they lack the personal touch of being in a room with your own sangha, there's often a good feeling about meditating together, and discussing your practice with others, even if you are physically far removed from them. If you can find a suitable dharma group some distance away, you might try commuting occasionally to meet with them, and perhaps attending their retreats. You might even consider moving closer to them! That's a bit drastic, but the reward is practising with like-minded people.

If all else fails – why not start your own group? This can begin as a few friends who wish to meditate together, or you could advertise in your local social media, making clear that this is an independent group, rather than a branch of Theravada, Tibetan or Zen Buddhism. You will probably need to practise for some time before you have the experience and the confidence to lead other people into meditation. The group may not turn out as you would wish. Perhaps the support may not be there, or people don't want to meet as often as you would like, or they want the group to be different. All these are excellent tests of your patience and perseverance. It's still worth trying, even if the group doesn't last – which only means it's as impermanent as everything else.

Building a Sangha

Leaving monastic traditions behind raises the question of how to practise within a new form of sangha. Individual unofficial Buddhists will need to find ways of meeting with other dharma practitioners, both formally and informally, and developing ways of mutual support in small, local sanghas not affiliated to traditional groups. Stephen Batchelor describes a secular sangha as 'a community of like-minded, self-reliant individuals, united by friendship'.[1] The members of these small groups will need to be committed and active rather than half-hearted and passive. They will be democratic groups with no formal teacher, though some members will inevitably be more experienced than others.

A new local group might begin by pooling their experience of practice to see which traditions are particularly valued, though personal preferences often need to give way to engage fully in a sangha. The more we can make the running of the group a collaborative exercise the better, both in terms of the effort individuals have to put in and the sense of commitment members of the group will feel. Taking turns to lead the group, members may choose to bring a short extract for reading and discussion – either from ancient scriptures or contemporary teachers – explaining what the text means to them and why they have brought it to the group.

A purely secular approach may be seen as too radical, and the new sangha might be looking for a compromise between secular Buddhism and an informal Theravada or Zen practice. Without a formal affiliation, individual groups can still benefit from the monastic traditions, perhaps even sometimes going on retreat at a Theravada, Tibetan or Zen centre.

Some writers have taken the use of *sangha* further to include all people in a particular community, or a particular country, and finally to refer loosely to all beings as members of the sangha we might call *earthlings* – whether human or non-human – hurtling through space on the same ball of rock. This wider usage reflects an awareness of our interdependence with one another, our connections with all beings, and our wish to look after them rather than to exploit them.

The Japanese Soto Zen priest Shohaku Okumura (b. 1948) argues that if we limit the use of *sangha* to our own little Buddhist group, it can become 'a sort of group ego'. Instead we should work for the good of all rather than for our individual benefit, avoiding the selfish attitude which divides our community into *us* and *them* and which can thus cause conflict. Without *sangha* as 'a living community of people', the Buddha is simply a figure from the past, with his teaching only 'something printed in a textbook'. The dharma only comes alive when there is a community to practice it in their daily lives. Okumura describes how our good friends in Buddhism include our dharma teachers, the people we practise with, and also everyone who supports our practice in one way or another. Perhaps we shouldn't think of our *sangha* as this small group sitting in silence together, but a much wider community, all caring for each other.[2]

The Zen master, poet and peace activist Thich Nhat Hanh (1926–2022) also saw the Buddhist sangha as part of a wider community – local and national and even international – coming together 'to pool our wisdom, our insight, and our compassion to build a lasting peace in the world'. Modern Western culture has often been dominated by individualism, but this ego-driven approach doesn't lead to harmony or happiness. Instead our practice needs to engage fully with society and culture, in order to 'bring the spiritual dimension to your daily life, to your social, political, and economic life'. He defined the essence of a true sangha as 'awareness, understanding, acceptance, harmony, and love'. That's why taking refuge in the sangha is such an important element of our practice, allowing us to be supported by like-minded friends, who will always help us when we are in difficulties. Of course we also need to support them. Sangha-building is a mutual process, where even the most difficult people need to be embraced with compassion.[3]

When asked what was the greatest happiness or blessing, the Buddha emphasized the virtues of skilful action, speech and livelihood which we have been discussing. But he also includes what we might call sangha-building:

> Not to associate with fools, but to associate with the wise and to honour those who are worthy of honour ... timely hearing of the Dhamma ... association with exemplars of the Dhamma-life and participation in religious discussions...this is ... great happiness ... the highest blessing.[4]

A Pattern of Practice

That leaves us with the question of putting all the elements of our practice together, which can be confusing. Buddhism is full of numbers! We've looked at the three characteristics, the four tasks, the four boundless states, the eightfold path, and Zen's ten precepts. But aren't these different ways of expressing the same thing – the Buddha's path of morality, meditation and wisdom?

Chapter 3 posed a series of questions about the possible development of Buddhism in Western countries, asking which teachings and practices might be emphasized, which scriptures and other narratives might be seen as central, how wisdom and compassion might be encouraged in personal practice, which ethical precepts might be adopted, and how new forms of practice groups might be established. As an example, some suggestions were offered as to how this might happen in Britain. Having looked in some detail at the various steps on the eightfold path, it may be helpful finally to step back and consider these broader questions again. As unofficial Buddhists, how should we relate to each of these elements in our own daily practice?

We've just looked at how we might practice together rather than on our own. But there's a lot more to think about here. Without the focus of monastery attendance for meditation, chanting and devotional practice, unofficial Buddhists need to find simpler forms for personal practice at home. This will certainly include daily meditation to develop calm and insight and compassion, using mindfulness of breathing, and perhaps loving-kindness or gratitude meditation, as described in Chapter 9. We may choose to offer candles and incense, to recite or chant some short verses to focus our attention before meditation, and perhaps even to renew our commitment to engage with the Zen precepts. (Suggestions for these verses are given in the Appendix.)

At the heart of our practice, instead of the Four Noble Truths as a set of beliefs, will be the fourfold task described in Chapter 1 – engaging with life and its problems, letting go of our habitual reactions, observing how they can fade, and cultivating the eightfold path of morality, meditation and wisdom. We may well envisage this as the Zen-based path described in Chapter 4 of ethical behaviour, meditation, developing compassion, and realizing (making real) our Buddha nature, our natural wisdom.

To support all this we'll still read about the life and teaching of the Buddha, and the later writings of teachers from different traditions. There are excellent modern translations of Theravada, Tibetan and Zen texts, but their sheer size can be overwhelming. The Buddha's discourses in the Pali canon cover nearly 5,000 pages, with 40 further volumes of texts, interpretative literature and the monastic code. This is before we come to the Chinese canon, the scriptures of Tibetan Buddhism, and many volumes of Zen writings, often seen as scriptures in their own right. Reading these texts reveals a great deal of repetition. It might be easier to build up a collection of passages we find illuminating, challenging or reassuring, and which will help with our own practice. Each of us will find different examples to inspire and guide us. Ask your friends. At our Zen group, we invite people to bring a passage to read, and we've all found new ideas and new writers this way. There are excellent anthologies such as Bhikkhu Bodhi's *In the Buddha's Words*, taken from the Pali canon, or the Zen writings in Tanahashi and Levitt's *The Essential Dogen*.[5] There's also much to read with benefit from Japanese writers such as D.T. Suzuki, Shunryu Suzuki Roshi and Taizan Maezumi Roshi, and from contemporary American and European teachers such as Charlotte Joko Beck, Norman Fischer, Diane Rizzetto, and Stephen and Martine Batchelor. And of course those who inspire us need not all be Buddhist writers!

Teachings and narratives have little resonance unless they touch the heart in some way. So we will try to use them to help us develop and practise the four boundless states of loving-kindness, compassion, equanimity and sympathetic joy. In both our formal meditation and our daily mindfulness, we will hope to be able to wish all beings well, and to generate positive feelings of gratitude and happiness towards them wherever we can.

Our exploration and practice of the ten Zen precepts will hopefully lead beyond refraining from killing and stealing, misusing the senses, lying and intoxication and so on – important though these are – and will prompt the development of the virtues of loving-kindness, generosity, contentment, truthfulness and mindfulness. This will help us eventually to express and promote concord, goodwill and wisdom.

We might also consider how to express our practice in visual terms, using whichever symbols of the dharma appear most appropriate for us. Perhaps you choose to have an altar with an image of the Buddha, offering candlelight and incense as you begin your meditation. You may also be inspired by the iconography of different Buddhist traditions – the restrained beauty of Thai temple paintings, the exuberant radiance of a Tibetan centre, or the subdued colours of a Zen monastery. Each of these has the power to touch the heart. On a pilgrimage in India, I visited the Sarnath museum, and was drawn back again and again to a famous sculpture of the preaching Buddha. Although slightly damaged, this sandstone figure had a remarkable effect, almost like standing in front of the Buddha himself, as he explained the dharma with a quiet radiance.

* * *

We've spent much of this book working out the difference between harmful and skilful actions, how to avoid the harmful and develop and practise the skilful, and how meditation can help us in this process of awakening the compassionate heart. This brings us back to the verse quoted in the Introduction, which I sometimes use to try to explain Buddhism to people. There's much more in this verse than at first appears. It looks so simple. Follow the precepts and be compassionate. But practising skilful actions goes far beyond exploring and following the precepts. It actually encompasses *all* the steps made by walking on the eightfold path. Our skilful action, speech and livelihood is supported by skilful understanding and thinking, developed by skilful effort, and surrounded by skilful meditation and mindfulness. The final line reminds us that the teaching is all here in a single verse:

Avoid all harmful actions of body, speech and mind
Practise skilful actions of body, speech and mind
Awaken your compassionate heart –
This is the teaching of the Buddhas.

Enjoy your practice. And don't forget that those skilful actions include regular meditation!

Appendix: Verses for Meditation and Reflection

There can still be a place for ceremonial in the lives of unofficial Buddhists. We may find it helpful to light candles and incense before meditation, and to recite some short verses. This expresses our commitment to follow the Buddha's teaching, and also helps to calm the mind. For example, we might chant the Buddha's *Words on Loving-Kindness* in the morning, and recite part of Dogen's *Recommending Zazen* in the evening.

Suggested verses are set out below. If you find any of these helpful, feel free to use or adapt them as you wish. Or you can choose verses from your own tradition. Whatever inspires us and reminds us of why we're walking on a spiritual path is worth reciting regularly. Appropriate language is helpful – but remember Dogen's warning: *stop chasing words and studying phrases. Learn to step back and reflect instead upon yourself.*

The Robe Verse

How great is the robe of awakening,
Formless, the field of happiness!
Unfold and wear the Buddha's teaching
To help all living beings.

The Robe Verse suggests that we wear the Buddha's teaching as if it were a robe which symbolizes *awakening*. A cotton plant becomes a piece of cloth, a robe, and then compost. With no fixed form, we may see it as *formless*, incapable of being held onto. We receive the teaching with open hands rather than grasping fingers. This is the field of our own body and mind, where we practice cultivating virtue or *happiness*. So we *unfold and wear the Buddha's teaching*, which protects us like a robe. And this is not just for ourselves: we cultivate this field *to help all living beings*.

Honouring the Three Treasures

We honour and respect the Buddha, who is our true teacher
We honour and respect the Dharma, the medicine for all suffering
We honour and respect the Sangha, the wise and compassionate

Honouring the Three Treasures reminds us to respect the person of the Buddha, the dharma of his teaching, and the sangha of all those who form the Buddhist community.

The Three Refuges

I take refuge in Buddha, the awakened potential of all beings
I take refuge in Dharma, the ocean of wisdom and compassion
I take refuge in Sangha, the interdependence of all beings

The Three Refuges represent a formal commitment, taking the Three Treasures as our guide, but in a much wider sense – Buddha as the potential for awakening, Dharma as wisdom and compassion wherever we find it, and Sangha as the connection between all living beings.

The Three Precepts

Avoid all harmful actions of body, speech and mind
Practise skilful actions of body, speech and mind
Awaken your compassionate heart –
This is the teaching of the Buddhas.

The Three Precepts summarizes our spiritual practice in a verse adapted from the *Dhammapada*.

From the Buddha's Words on Loving-Kindness

This is what should be done
By one who is skilled in goodness,
And who knows the path of peace:

Let them be able and upright,
Straightforward and gentle in speech,
Humble and not conceited,
Contented and easily satisfied,
Unburdened with duties, and frugal in their ways.
Peaceful and calm, and wise and skilful,
Not proud and demanding in nature.

Let them not do the slightest thing
That the wise would later reprove,
Wishing: In gladness and in safety –
May all beings be at ease!

Whatever living beings there may be,
Whether they are weak or strong, omitting none,
The great or the mighty, medium, short or small,
Those living near and far away,
Those born and to-be-born –
May all beings be at ease!

Let none deceive another,
Or despise any being in any state.
Let none through anger or ill-will
Wish harm upon another.

Even as a mother protects with her life
Her child, her only child,
So with a boundless heart
Should one cherish all living beings,
Radiating kindness over the entire world:
Spreading upwards to the skies
And downwards to the depths,
Outwards and unbounded,
Freed from hatred and ill-will.

Recommending Zazen: Meditation for All

The complete way flows everywhere: what use is practice and awakening? The essential teaching is freely available: how could effort be needed? The dharma is always right where you are: why wander off to search for it?

Yet the way is as distant as heaven from earth, if the mind is lost in the confusion of likes and dislikes. You may be proud of your understanding, but if your mind is still wandering, you have almost lost the way to awakening.

Consider the Buddha's great wisdom, and the influence of his six years in meditation. Remember how Bodhidharma spent nine years facing a wall. Who nowadays does not need to practice like these ancient sages?

So stop chasing words and studying phrases. Learn to step back and reflect instead upon yourself. Body and mind will fall away and your original face will appear. If you want to find this, practise this without delay.

Take your meditation seat in a quiet room. Wear loose clothing and arrange it neatly. Put aside all activities, all the conscious mind's reflections about good and bad, right and wrong. Rest one hand in the palm of the other. Sit upright with your head and body centred. Sway your body left and right, then breathe in deeply and breathe out fully. Now sit still like a mountain, neither thinking nor not thinking. How do you think of not thinking? Beyond thinking. This is the very basis of zazen.

This zazen is not learning to concentrate. It is simply the dharma-gate of peace and happiness, the practice-realization of complete awakening, free from the web of confusion. Once you experience this, you will see that the dharma appears naturally, clearing darkness and distraction from the mind.

So do not worry about how intelligent you are, how dull or sharp-witted. Practise wholeheartedly: your single-minded effort is itself the way. Why leave your own seat to wander away? Even one wrong step leads you away from the present moment.

You have received a precious human life: do not waste your time. What use are fleeting pleasures? Our life is like a flash of lightning, transient and illusory – suddenly it is gone.

Dear Zen practitioners, do not grasp at appearance, do not be scared of reality. Devote your energy to this direct and straightforward way. Become one with the awakened wisdom of the Buddhas, and receive their peaceful inheritance.

Dedications

May I/you/all beings be free from suffering and the roots of suffering!
May my heart/your hearts/their hearts be filled with loving-kindness!
May I/you/all beings be peaceful and at ease!
May I/you/all beings be well! May I/you/all beings be happy!

After meditation we might express a wish for our own well-being, then for our teachers and friends, our family and neighbours, and finally a wish that all beings may be free from suffering, peaceful and happy.

Renewal Days

On new moon and full moon days, Buddhist monks and nuns recite their precepts and reflect on them. These *Renewal Days* may help to remind us of our own practice. So the *Renewal Verse* can remind us of the fourfold task the Buddha invites us to engage with. We can also acknowledge our mistakes, being aware of our limitations, and looking forward to a *turning around*, a change of direction. Reciting the Ten Great Precepts slowly brings to mind in turn each of the harmful actions, the habitual negative reactions we wish to abandon, and each of the skilful actions of body, speech and mind we wish to develop.

The Renewal Verse

May the Buddha's teaching guide us –
To embrace life and its suffering
To let go of our habitual reactions
To see how these reactions can fade
And to cultivate the eightfold path.

All my repeated unwholesome actions are born
From beginningless greed, hate and delusion.
All the wrong is done by my body, speech and mind
Aware of my imperfections, I vow to start again.

May this act of recognition bring a change of heart
Aware of my imperfections, and awakening my compassionate heart,
    I vow to start again.

The Ten Great Precepts

Letting go of the wish to harm others, I take up the way of loving-kindness, supporting and protecting living beings.

Letting go of selfish greed, I take up the way of generosity, the way of giving freely all that I can.

Letting go of selfish sensuality, I take up the way of contentment, self-restraint and faithfulness, treating all beings with respect and dignity.

Letting go of deceitful speech, I take up the way of truthfulness, listening and speaking from the heart.

Letting go of intoxicants and delusive thinking, I take up the way of mindfulness, the way of cultivating a clear mind.

Letting go of harsh and divisive speech, I take up the way of kindly and gentle speech, the way of promoting concord.

Letting go of praising myself and maliciously blaming others, I take up the way of meeting others on equal ground.

Letting go of stinginess, I take up the way of freely offering spiritual or material help to all those who are in need.

Letting go of harbouring anger and ill-will, I take up the way of compassion, offering goodwill and friendship to all living beings.

Letting go of false views, I take up the way of honouring and respecting buddha, dharma and sangha, the way of cultivating wisdom.

Notes

Introduction

1. *Anguttara Nikaya* 3:53. Bodhi (2012), p. 251.
2. *Dhammapada*, verse 183. Dhammapada quotations have been compiled from several different translations.
3. Antonio Machado, 'Proverbs and Songs' XXIX, in *Fields of Castile* (1917) (compiled from several translations).

1 Four Truths – or Four Tasks?

1. *Anguttara Nikaya* 3:65. Bodhi (2012), p. 280-1.
2. *Anguttara Nikaya* 3:53. Bodhi (2012), p. 251.
3. Conze (1980), p. 21.
4. *Samyutta Nikaya* 56:11. Bodhi (2000), p. 1844.
5. *Samyutta Nikaya* 56:11. Bodhi (2000), p. 1844-5.
6. Batchelor (2015), ix.
7. Batchelor (2015), p. 20.
8. Batchelor (2015), p. 21.
9. Ling (1973), pp. 17, 22.
10. Batchelor (2015), p. 27.
11. *Anguttara Nikaya*, 3:55. Bodhi (2012), p. 253.
12. Batchelor (2019), 'Unit 3: Letting Go of Reactivity'.
13. Batchelor (2015), p. 79.
14. Batchelor (2015), p. 86.
15. Batchelor (2015), p. 122.
16. Batchelor (2015), pp. 313-14.
17. Batchelor (2015), p. 316.

2 Looking for the Middle Way

1. Pym (2001), p. 7.
2. *Anguttara Nikaya* 3:65. Bodhi (2012), p. 281

3. Willmer (1995).
4. Batchelor (2015), p. 20.
5. *Digha Nikaya* 16:1. Walshe (1995), p. 231f.
6. Batchelor (2015), p. 315.
7. MacPhillamy (2003), p. 139.
8. Maezumi Roshi (2002), xi.

3 Finding a Local Path

1. Fischer (2017).
2. see Bluck (2006), p. 191f
3. Humphreys (1968), p. 8.
4. Humphreys (1968), p. 80.
5. *Majjhima Nikaya* 139:3. Ñanamoli and Bodhi (1995), p. 1080.
6. Subharo (2019).

4 Towards a Zen Path?

1. Ling (1973), pp. 122, 238–9.
2. *Digha Nikaya* 31:27–33. Walshe (1995), pp. 466–8.
3. Fischer and Moon (2016), p. 54.
4. Suzuki (1991), pp. 38–40, 45
5. Suzuki (2010), p. 1.
6. Suzuki (2010), p. 62.
7. Chadwick (2021), p.18.
8. Kapleau (1980b), pp. 171, 196, 200, 270.
9. Humphreys (1981), pp. 179–80.
10. Gabb (1956), pp. 48–9.
11. Kennett (1999), p. 14.
12. MacPhillamy (ed.) (2000), p. 20.
13. MacPhillamy (ed.) (2000), xxiv.
14. MacPhillamy (2003), p. 124.
15. Fischer and Moon (2016), pp. 1–2
16. Dogen, 'Recommending Zazen: Meditation for All' (compiled from several translations). See Appendix.
17. Ibid.
18. Fischer and Moon (2016), pp. 31–3.
19. Fischer and Moon (2016), p. 93.
20. *Samyutta Nikaya* 36:21. Bodhi (2000), p. 1279.
21. Fischer and Moon (2016), p. 60.
22. Suzuki (1991), p. 40; Kapleau (1980a), p. 31.
23. Fischer and Moon (2016), pp. 81–2.

24. Uchiyama (2004), xxx.
25. Fischer and Moon (2016), p. 178.

5 Taking the First Steps

1. Gunaratana (2001).
2. Ling (1970), p. 19.
3. Gunaratana (2001), p. 27.
4. *Dhammapada*, verses 1–2 (compiled from several translations).
5. *Majjhima Nikaya* 9:4–8, 41:7–14. Ñanamoli and Bodhi (1995), pp. 132–3, 380–3.
6. *Dhammapada*, verse 276 (compiled from several translations).
7. *Majjhima Nikaya* 117:11. Ñanamoli and Bodhi (1995), p. 935.
8. Gampopa (1995), pp. 92–5.
9. Amaravati (1994), p. 37. This translation of the Metta Sutta is also available at www.accesstoinsight.org/tipitaka/kn/khp/khp9.amar.html. See also Appendix.
10. *Samyutta Nikaya* 22:15. Bodhi (2000), p. 869 (slightly adapted).
11. Batchelor et al (2020). 'Unit 2: Wise View and Wise Intention'.
12. Batchelor and Batchelor (2019), 'Unit 1: What is Secular Dharma?'

6 Cultivating Compassionate Behaviour

1. Amaravati (1994), p. 36. See also Appendix.
2. *Digha Nikaya* 31:27–33. Walshe (1995), pp. 466–8.
3. Rizzetto (2005), pp. 10, 18.
4. *Dhammapada*, verse 131 (compiled from several translations).
5. Shantideva (1997), p. 123.
6. Amaravati (1994), p. 37. See also Appendix.
7. Gampopa (1995), pp. 98–9.
8. Rizzetto (2006), p. 19.
9. Rizzetto (2006), pp. 111, 118.
10. *Anguttara Nikaya* 4:61. Bodhi (2012), p. 450.
11. Anderson (2001), p. 112.
12. Dogen, 'Recommending Zazen: Meditation for All' (compiled from several translations). See Appendix.
13. Amaravati (1994), p. 36. See also Appendix.
14. *Majjhima Nikaya* 22:13–14. Ñanamoli and Bodhi (1995), pp. 228–9.

7 The Power of Speech

1. *Majjhima Nikaya* 41:9, 41.13. Ñanamoli and Bodhi (1995), pp. 380–3.
2. *Digha Nikaya* 1:1.9. Walshe (1995), pp. 68–9. (This whole passage on moral behaviour is repeated in the next twelve suttas in the *Digha Nikaya*.)

3. *Majjhima Nikaya* 114:6. Ñanamoli and Bodhi (1995), p. 916.
4. Ibid.
5. Ibid., pp. 915-6.
6. Rizzetto (2006), pp. 71-2.
7. Anderson (2001), pp. 151, 156.
8. Rizzetto (2006), p. 82.

8 And What Do You Do for a Living?

1. *Digha Nikaya* 31:7-13, 31:32. Walshe (1995), pp. 462-3, 468.
2. Schumacher (1974), pp. 44-51.
3. Amaravati (1994), p. 36. See also Appendix.
4. *Samyutta Nikaya* 42:12. Bodhi (2000), p. 1352.

9 Focusing on the Present

1. Dogen, 'Recommending Zazen: Meditation for All' (compiled from several translations). See Appendix.
2. *Majjhima Nikaya* 141:29. Ñanamoli and Bodhi (1995), p. 1100.
3. Armstrong (2011), p. 69: see Bodhi (2000), p. 869 (slightly adapted).
4. *Majjhima Nikaya* 39:14. Ñanamoli and Bodhi (1995), pp. 366-7.
5. Gunaratana (2001), p. 188-9.
6. *Majjhima Nikaya* 10. Ñanamoli and Bodhi (1995), pp. 145-55.
7. MacPhillamy (2003), p. 58-9.
8. Amaravati (1994), p. 36-7. See also Appendix.

10 Skilful Meditation

1. Fontana (2004), p. 12.
2. *Digha Nikaya* 2:75-81. Walshe (1995) pp. 102-3.
3. Chodron (2002).
4. Fontana (2004), p. 14.
5. In Chadwick (2021), p. 53.
6. Dogen, 'Recommending Zazen: Meditation for All' (compiled from several translations). See Appendix.
7. In Chadwick (2021), pp. 6, 35.
8. Amaravati (1994), p. 37. See also Appendix.
9. Ibid.
10. Ibid.

11 A Path towards Wisdom?

1. Eliot (1963), 'Choruses from "The Rock"', I, p. 161.
2. MacPhillamy (2003), p. 36.
3. *Samyutta Nikaya* 12:65. Bodhi (2000), p. 603.
4. Batchelor (2015), p. 312.
5. *Anguttara Nikaya* 3:102. Bodhi (2012), p. 338.
6. Anderson (2001), p. 174.
7. Rizzetto (2006), pp. 143, 148–9.
8. Ling (1973), pp. 112–14.

12 All Together Now

1. Batchelor (2015), p. 316.
2. Okumura (2012), pp. 36, 71, 73–4.
3. Nhat Hanh (2002), pp. 16, 18.
4. Saddhatissa (1985), pp. 29–30.
5. Bodhi (2005); Tanahashi (2013).

Bibliography

This list includes works quoted and those consulted. Buddhist texts have been referenced using both the original texts and their translators, but are listed here only under their translators. I have avoided diacritics in Pali and Sanskrit terms, for the sake of clarity, consistency and ease of reproduction.

Amaravati. (1994). *Chanting Book: Morning and Evening Puja and Reflections*. Hemel Hempstead: Amaravati Publications.
Anderson, Reb. (2001). *Being Upright: Zen Meditation and the Bodhisattva Precepts*. Berkeley, California: Rodmell Press.
Armstrong, Karen. (2011). *Twelve Steps to a Compassionate Life*. London: Bodley Head.
Batchelor, Martine. (2010). *The Spirit of the Buddha*. New Haven, Connecticut: Yale University Press.
Batchelor, Stephen. (2015). *After Buddhism: Rethinking the Dharma for a Secular Age*. New Haven, Connecticut: Yale University Press.
Batchelor, Stephen and Martine. (2019). *Secular Dharma*. (Tricycle Online Course)
Batchelor et al. (2020). *Reimagining the Eightfold Path*. (Tricycle Online Course)
Beck, Charlotte Joko. (1997). *Everyday Zen: Love and Work*. London: Thorsons.
Beck, Charlotte Joko. (2021). *Ordinary Wonder: Zen Life and Practice* (ed. Brenda Beck Hess). Boulder, Colorado: Shambhala.
Bluck, Robert. (2006). *British Buddhism: Teachings, Practice and Development*. Abingdon: Routledge.
Bodhi, Bhikkhu. (2000). *The Connected Discourses of the Buddha: A New Translation of the Samyutta Nikaya*. Somerville, Massachusetts: Wisdom Publications.
Bodhi, Bhikkhu (ed.). (2005). *In the Buddha's Words: An Anthology of Discourses from the Pali Canon*. Somerville, Massachusetts: Wisdom Publications.
Bodhi, Bhikkhu. (2012). *The Numerical Discourses of the Buddha: A Translation of the Anguttara Nikaya*. Somerville, Massachusetts: Wisdom Publications.
Buxton, Nicholas. (2020). *Just Meditation: Everyday Meditation for Everyone*. Durham: Magic Monastery Publishing.

Chadwick, David (ed.). (2021). *Zen is Right Now: More Teaching Stories and Anecdotes of Shunryu Suzuki*. Boulder, Colorado: Shambhala.

Chodron, Pema. (2002). '5 Reasons to Meditate'. *Lion's Roar* (March), n.p..

Conze, Edward. (1980). *A Short History of Buddhism*. London: George Allen & Unwin.

Eliot, T.S. (1963). *Collected Poems 1909-1962*. London: Faber and Faber.

Ellis, Robert M. (2019). *The Buddha's Middle Way: Experiential Judgement in his Life and Teaching*. Sheffield: Equinox.

Fischer, Norman. (2017). 'Buddhism's New Pioneers'. *Lion's Roar.* (November), n.p.

Fischer, Norman and Moon, Susan. (2016). *What is Zen? Plain Talk for a Beginner's Mind*. Boulder, Colorado: Shambhala.

Fontana, David. (2004). *Meditation Week by Week: 52 Meditations to Help You Grow in Peace*. London: Duncan Baird.

Gabb, W.J. (1956). *The Goose is Out*. London: Buddhist Society.

Gampopa, Je. (1995). *Gems of Dharma, Jewels of Freedom: Clear and Authoritative Classic Handbook of Mahayana Buddhism by the Great 12th Century Tibetan Bodhisattva* (trans. Ken and Katia Holmes). London: Altea Publishing.

Gunaratana, Henepola. (2001). *Eight Mindful Steps to Happiness: Walking the Buddha's Path*. Somerville, Massachusetts: Wisdom Publications.

Harvey, Peter (2000). *Introduction to Buddhist Ethics: Foundations, Values and Issues*. Cambridge: Cambridge University Press.

Harvey, Peter (2013). *An Introduction to Buddhism: Teachings, History and Practices*. Second edition. Cambridge: Cambridge University Press.

Humphreys, Christmas. (1968). *Sixty Years of Buddhism in England*. London: Buddhist Society.

Humphreys, Christmas. (1981). *Buddhism* (first published 1951). Harmondsworth: Penguin.

Kapleau, Roshi Philip. (1980a) *The Three Pillars of Zen: Teaching, Practice, and Enlightenment* (first published 1965). London: Rider.

Kapleau, Roshi Philip. (1980b). *Zen: Dawn in the West* (first published 1978). London: Rider.

Katagiri, Dainin. (1988). *Returning to Silence: Zen Practice in Everyday Life*. Boulder, Colorado: Shambhala.

Kennett, Roshi P.T.N.H. (1999). *Zen is Eternal Life* (first published 1972 as *Selling Water by the River*). Mt Shasta, California: Shasta Abbey Press.

Ling, Trevor. (1970). *Buddhism*. London: Ward Lock Educational.

Ling, Trevor. (1973). *The Buddha: Buddhist Civilization in India and Ceylon*. London: Temple Smith.

MacPhillamy, Rev. Daizui (ed.). (2000). *Roar of the Tigress: The Oral Teachings of Rev. Master Jiyu-Kennett: Western Woman and Zen Master. Volume 1: An*

Introduction to Zen: Religious Practice for Everyday Life. Mt Shasta, California: Shasta Abbey Press.

MacPhillamy, Rev. Daizui. (2003). *Buddhism from Within: An Intuitive Introduction to Buddhism*. Mt Shasta, California: Shasta Abbey Press.

Maezumi Roshi, Taizan. (2002). *Appreciate Your Life: The Essence of Zen Practice*. Boulder, Colorado: Shambhala.

Maezumi Roshi, Taizan and Glassman, Bernie (eds.). (2002). *On Zen Practice: Body, Breath, Mind*. Somerville, Massachusetts: Wisdom Publications.

Ñanamoli, Bhikkhu and Bodhi, Bhikkhu. (1995). *The Middle Length Discourses of the Buddha: A New Translation of the Majjhima Nikāya*. Somerville, Massachusetts: Wisdom Publications.

Nhat Hanh, Thich. (2002). *Friends on the Path: Living Spiritual Communities*. Berkeley, California: Parallax Press.

Okumura, Shohaku. (2012). *Living by Vow: A Practical Introduction to Eight Essential Zen Chants and Texts*. Somerville, Massachusetts: Wisdom Publications.

Pym, Jim. (2001). *You Don't Have to Sit on the Floor*. London: Rider.

Rahula, Walpola. (1959). *What the Buddha Taught*. London: Gordon Fraser.

Rizzetto, Diane Eshin. (2006). *Waking Up to What You Do: A Zen Practice for Meeting Every Situation with Intelligence and Compassion*. Boulder, Colorado: Shambhala.

Saddhatissa, H. (1985). *The Sutta-Nipāta*. London: Curzon Press.

Schumacher. E.F (1974). *Small Is Beautiful: A Study of Economics as if People Mattered*. London: Abacus.

Shantideva. (1997). *The Way of the Bodhisattva* (Padmakara Translation Group). Boulder, Colorado: Shambhala.

Subharo, Ajahn. (2019). 'Majjhima Nikaya Favorites part 2' (https://bhikkhu.ca/suttas/2019/03/22/Majjhima-Nikaya-Favorites-part-2.html)

Suzuki, D.T. (1991). *An Introduction to Zen Buddhism* (first published 1934). London: Rider.

Suzuki, Shunryu. (2010). *Zen Mind, Beginner's Mind: Informal Talks on Zen Meditation and Practice*. Fortieth Anniversary Edition (first published 1970). Boulder, Colorado: Shambhala.

Tanahashi, Kazuaki and Levitt, Peter (eds.). (2013). *The Essential Dogen: Writings of the Great Zen Master*. Boulder, Colorado: Shambhala.

Uchiyama, Kosho. (2004). *Opening the Hand of Thought: Foundations of Zen Buddhist Practice*. Somerville, Massachusetts: Wisdom Publications.

Walshe, Maurice (1995). *The Long Discourses of the Buddha: A Translation of the Digha Nikaya* (first published 1987). Somerville, Massachusetts: Wisdom Publications.

Willmer, Haddon. (1995). 'Obituary: Professor Trevor Ling'. *The Independent*, 15 June.

www.ingramcontent.com/pod-product-compliance
Lightning Source LLC
Chambersburg PA
CBHW062012180426
43199CB00034B/2505